DECORATING
CERAMICS

DECORATING CERAMICS

OVER 300 EASY-TO-PAINT PATTERNS

NICKY COONEY

Sterling Publishing Co., Inc.
New York
A Sterling/Silver Book

A QUARTO BOOK

Library of Congress Cataloging-in-Publication Data is available upon request.

Published by Sterling Publishing Company Inc
387 Park Avenue South
New York, NY 10016

This book was designed and produced by
Quarto Publishing plc
The Old Brewery
6 Blundell Street
London N7 9BH

Project Editor Marnie Haslam
Editor Mike Stocks
Art Editor Sally Bond
Picture Researcher Gill Metcalf, Marnie Haslam
Designer Karin Skånberg
Assistant Art Director Penny Cobb
Photographer Colin Bowling
Illustrator Nicky Cooney
Art Director Moira Clinch
QUART.ELD

Manufactured by Eray Scan Pte Ltd, Singapore
Printed by Star Standard Industries (Pte) Ltd, Singapore

ISBN 0-8069-6325-5

CONTENTS

- INTRODUCTION **6**
- GETTING READY **8**
- USING THE TEMPLATES **12**
- TECHNIQUES **14**
- DESIGNS IN COLOR **23**

PROJECTS
ROUNDED CUP & SAUCER 1 **24**
ROUNDED CUP & SAUCER 2 **26**
STRAIGHT-SIDED CUP & SAUCER **28**
STRAIGHT-SIDED MUG **30**
CURVED MUG **32**
- CONE MUG **34**
- STRAIGHT-SIDED BEAKER **36**
- ROUND SUGAR BOWL **38**
- LIPPED BOWL **40**
- UNLIPPED BOWL **42**

CONE BOWL **44**
LARGE SALAD/FRUIT BOWL **46**
LARGE, SHALLOW BOWL **48**
SMALL JUG **50**
LARGE JUG **52**
STRAIGHT-SIDED JUG **54**
ROUND TEAPOT 1 **56**
ROUND TEAPOT 2 **58**
STRAIGHT-SIDED TEAPOT **60**
STRAIGHT-SIDED COFFEE POT **62**
SAUCE/GRAVY BOAT & SAUCER **64**

SMALL, CURVED VASE **66**
LARGE, CURVED VASE **68**
CONE VASE **70**
OTHER TALL, SHAPED VASES **72**
PLANTER **74**
EGGCUP **76**
SALT AND PEPPER CRUET SET **78**
MUSTARD POT **80**
SMALL, LIDDED STORAGE/SPICE JAR **82**
LARGE, LIDDED STORAGE/SPICE JAR **84**
BUTTER DISH **86**
CHEESE DISH **88**
ROUND VEGETABLE TUREEN **90**
LARGE ROASTING DISH **92**

SMALL, ROUND PLATE **94**
MEDIUM, ROUND PLATE **96**
LARGE, ROUND PLATE **98**
SMALL, MEDIUM, & LARGE, SQUARE PLATES **100**
HEXAGONAL PLATES **102**
ROUND SERVING DISH/PLATTER **104**
OVAL SERVING DISH/PLATTER **106**
SQUARE SERVING DISH/PLATTER **108**
RECTANGULAR/ HEXAGONAL SERVING DISH **110**
SQUARE TILES/ COASTERS **112**
OTHER SHAPES OF TILES/COASTERS **114**

THEMES

1 CELEBRATIONS **116**
2 ASTROLOGY/NEW AGE **118**
3 ALPHABETS/LETTERING **120**
4 ANIMALS **122**
5 FLOWERS, FRUIT & VEG **124**

SUPPLIERS **126**
INDEX **127**
CREDITS **128**

INTRODUCTION

CERAMIC PAINTING *can provide hours of pleasure and the joy of creating your own unique masterpiece. This book contains over four hundred exciting designs for beginners and more advanced painters to copy or simply use as inspiration. Let your imagination run wild!*

In the following pages we will explain the simple techniques used to achieve these various designs and provide you with a list of materials and equipment you will need with the types of paints used in ceramic decoration. You will then be able to apply these designs to any number of glazed ceramics which are commercially available in so many different shapes and styles. By following the step-by-step instructions in the Techniques section, you will learn precisely how to transfer your favorite designs onto the objects of your choice. You might want to take a design shown on one type of object (a bowl, perhaps) and put it on another shape (a mug, for example), Sometimes this can present a few difficulties, but with a bit of creative innovation you can usually adapt or reproduce the original design in a unique new way. You will find there is at least one very simple design provided for every ceramic shape for those just learning the craft.

These days we are bombarded by visual images, from billboards, magazines, movies, and television to fabrics, graphic arts, fine arts, and much more. Whether we are visiting the museum, gazing at the stars, travelling through a beautiful landscape, or simply admiring some pretty flowers in a garden, these sources of inspiration are all around us. These are constant elements in

▲ *You can decorate almost any ceramic object with your own design, from plates to jars and vases.*

▶ *Musée Quai d'Orsay, Paris There is always plenty to see and inspire us in an art gallery or museum from ancient Chinese wall hangings to the dream-like oil paintings of Van Gogh.*

 ▶ *Hong Kong, Causway Bay*
These vibrantly colored neon
signs and billboards are excellent
examples of society's use of color
to catch the eye.

our daily lives which we can incorporate into original ceramic designs. Perhaps the designs in this book will inspire you to create your own designs in the future.

Conceiving original ideas requires patience and discipline, and, unfortunately, can also be time consuming. By providing you with over four hundred designs, this book makes the decorating process not just exciting and creative, but quick and simple too. And if, in the end, you do not feel inspired to create your own designs, you will find this book is a wonderful source of ideas.

However far you go in the art of ceramic decoration, whether you are content to decorate a single cup with a simple design from this book, or whether you progress to original and

complicated designs for complete sets of crockery, there is no doubt that you will find the activity rewarding and enjoyable.

By introducing you to the basic ceramic decorating techniques—eliminating most of the technical aspects and concentrating on the art of decoration—we hope you will be inspired to many hours of creative ceramic painting.

 ◀ *Lily Acapulco*
Sometimes artistic
inspiration can be no further than
your own backyard. The dazzling
beauty and profusion of nature
should provide you with endless
design ideas.

GETTING READY

A WORD OF *caution regarding paints: always read the manufacturer's instructions on the paint container, especially if the decorated area of your ceramic object is going to come into contact with food or drink or the mouth. The technology of paint safety is a constantly evolving field, and only the manufacturer's instructions will be up to date and accurate. The only definite way of making sure that a decorated piece is food safe is to fire it in a kiln at a higher temperature than a domestic oven can provide. You could consider approaching a local potter or college if you want your pieces to be fired at these higher temperatures. The alternative is to make sure that the contact area isn't decorated. For example, the rims of cups and mugs and pitchers should be paint-free, while for plates and dishes the paint should be confined to the sides, rims, and lids. Don't take any risks where there might be possible contact with food.*

TYPES OF PAINT

There are two types of paint used for ceramic decoration: water based and solvent based. The paints used for the designs in this book are water based. Water-based paints have a brighter finish than solvent-based ones, but their color range is more limited. They are diluted with water and dry in about four hours. The ceramic piece should then be baked in a domestic oven for twenty-four hours to increase its durability.

It is worth baking a test piece of ceramic, such as an old tile or a plate, before you put your new creation in the oven, to see if the temperature is accurate. If the temperature is too high, the colors will discolor; if it is too low the colors won't harden; and if you haven't allowed the paint to dry properly prior to baking, the paint will blister.

The oven should be pre-heated to 400°F (205°C) or gas mark 6 for ten minutes. Before putting your object into the oven, reduce the heat to 300°F (150°C) or gas mark 2. Bake the piece for thirty minutes and then remove it from the oven and allow it to cool.

Solvent-based paints have a wider color range than water-based paints and are diluted with turpentine. They do take longer to dry, usually about twenty-four hours. With this paint it is possible to add a clear glaze over the decoration, providing further protection for the design.

If you are decorating a lot of ceramics, you may want to invest in your own kiln. Electric kilns are available as either top-loading models (right) or with a front-opening door, but the latter are generally larger and more expensive.

Full-size kilns can fire a lot of items at once, placed on shelves separated by props. If you are loading the shelves, remember to put the heavier ceramics at the bottom.

It is a good idea to bake some test tiles first, so that you can see how the colors and finishes of your paints and glazes respond to different temperatures.

There are two types of paint used for ceramic decoration: water based and solvent based. Water-based paints have the advantage that they are easier to use and dry more quickly; however the colors are more limited. Solvent-based paints have stronger colors and are more durable, but they can take twenty-four hours to dry, and brushes must be cleaned in turpentine.

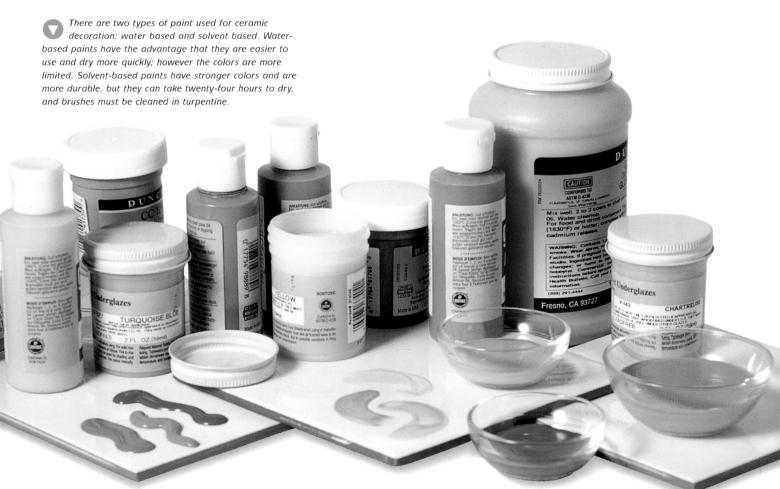

MATERIALS AND EQUIPMENT

You will be able to relax and enjoy your time painting ceramics if you are organized and plan your design in advance. Here are some of the materials you will need to get the best results. Most items should be readily available at your local craft store.

1 AIRTIGHT NON-POROUS CONTAINERS

These are useful for storing paint colors which you have already mixed. Glass jars are best as you can instantly see their contents, but containers which once contained food or beauty products are also suitable if thoroughly washed. Remember to label containers clearly, to close the lids firmly, and to keep them out of the reach of children.

2 BRUSHES

Brushes come in a variety of shapes and sizes for painting ceramics. You will need fine brushes for detailed work and larger brushes for bigger areas. You might find it useful to have a couple of differently sized brushes with oblique edges, because these are good for painting letters and numbers.

Pure sable brushes are the very best and consequently the most expensive. Nowadays there are also sable/synthetic mix brushes which retain many of the good qualities of sable but at more reasonable prices. Buy the best you can afford. It pays to take care of your brushes, because then they will last longer. Clean them thoroughly when changing from one color to another, and always clean them at the end of the day when you have finished using them.

3 ADHESIVE TAPE

Required for sticking carbon paper and stencils to ceramic objects.

4 CARBON PAPER

This is essential for transferring the designs onto the ceramic object. Although it usually comes in dark colors, white carbon is available for use on dark-colored ceramics.

5 COMPASSES

A necessary piece of equipment for drawing accurate circles.

6 COTTON SWABS

Useful for cleaning up paint edges.

7 CUTTING BOARD OR MAT

This will protect your work surface when cutting out stencils or masking film.

8 FIBER-TIPPED PEN

A non-waterproof pen for marking designs on your ceramic shape.

9 GRAPH PAPER

For increasing or decreasing the size of a design to fit your chosen object.

10 MASKING FILM, FLUID, OR TAPE

Keeps chosen areas on your ceramic object free from paint.

11 METHYLATED SPIRIT

Wiping the surface of your ceramic shape with this before you start painting insures that it is clean and grease free.

12 MODELING CLAY

Used for holding your ceramic shape in position on a turntable if continuous bands of color are required on a design.

13 PALETTE

You will need one of these for mixing your colors. An old white plate, saucer, or tile will do, or you can buy a custom-made plastic palette

14 PENCILS

Soft pencils such as 2Bs or 4Bs are used for marking directly onto the ceramic shape. An HB is useful for transferring designs from carbon paper to the ceramic or stencil paper.

15 RULER

Essential for precise measuring, the ruler should preferably be metal, giving a firm edge when cutting out either stencils or masking film.

16 SCALPEL

This is an excellent tool for accurately cutting out stencils. Make sure that you change the blades often enough; blunted blades make cutting more difficult and can be dangerous.

17 SKETCH PAD

A sketch pad is very useful for figuring out the order in which you want to apply the colors of a design, and for sizing designs up or down to fit the object you wish to decorate.

18 SCISSORS

Useful for cutting out simple shapes.

19 SPONGE

Handy for creating different paint effects.

20 STENCIL CARDBOARD

Essential for creating designs on the ceramics, stencil cardboard is particularly useful for repeat patterns.

21 STRING

Useful when marking up circular objects.

22 TAPE MEASURE

For measuring curved forms.

23 TISSUE

For cleaning up paint overspills and for creating paint effects

24 TOOTHBRUSH

For creating spattered effects—make sure it's an old one!

25 TRACING PAPER

Used in conjunction with carbon paper to transfer designs onto ceramics.

26 TURNTABLE

Sometimes referred to as a banding wheel, it is particularly useful when bands of color are needed on either hollow or flat ceramics.

27 TURPENTINE

Useful for thinning and wiping away excess solvent-based paint

USING THE TEMPLATES

TEMPLATES ARE *used for re-sizing designs (up or down, as required) and for transferring designs from the page to the object being decorated.*

RE-SIZING THE DESIGNS UP OR DOWN

There are two ways to approach the re-sizing of designs. The easy way is to use a photocopier. When photocopying your chosen design, use the zoom panel to either increase or decrease the size of the design. You may need to experiment a few times to get the exact size you need.

The other way of re-sizing is the traditional method of using a grid. Trace your chosen design from the book onto a piece of tracing paper. On the reverse of the tracing paper, trace the image again with a soft pencil. Turn the tracing paper over again and place it on a sheet from your sketch pad. Trace over the design a final time, using a hard pencil or a biro. Now remove the tracing paper, and you will be left with the design on the paper. Draw a grid of squares (A) over the design.

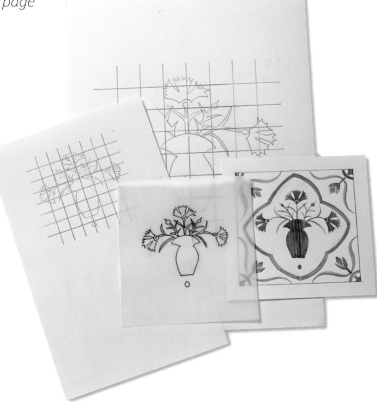

▲ *If you don't have access to a photocopier, use the traditional grid method—all you need is some tracing paper and a pencil.*

▲ *The easiest way to re-size your chosen design is to use a photocopier to enlarge or reduce your original.*

On another piece of tracing paper draw a second grid (B). It is very important that this second grid contains the same number of squares as the first one; however, the squares will be larger or smaller, depending on whether you want to increase or decrease the size of the design. To double the size of a design you would double the size of the squares. For example, if grid A comprised squares of 1 inch by 1 inch (2.5 cm by 2.5 cm), then grid B would comprise squares of 2 inches by 2 inches (5 cm by 5 cm). If you want to reduce the size of the design by half, then grid B would have squares of ½ inch by ½ inch (1.3 cm by 1.3 cm).

Now you have to copy the design in grid A into the squares of grid B. Start by noting where the gridlines of grid A are crossed by the lines of the image; carefully mark the gridlines of grid B in the same places, taking account of the difference in scale. Then draw the image one square at a time, checking it against the original to make sure you are being accurate.

These transfer techniques don't just apply to images—you can also use them to transfer lettering of all different styles. This is especially useful when the design is quite complex.

TRANSFERRING THE DESIGN

Once the design is the size you want, trace it onto a piece of tracing paper. Then take a piece of carbon paper and tape it into position on your ceramic object, inked side down. Place the tracing paper over the carbon paper and tape that down too. Trace over the design with a hard point such as a biro or a hard pencil, so that the design is transferred firmly onto the surface of the ceramic.

Gently remove both the tracing paper and the carbon paper. You might find it necessary to go over the outline carefully, using a fine marker pen, just to make the design more prominent. If the design you have chosen is complicated, it might be necessary to break it down into its constituent parts in order to transfer it.

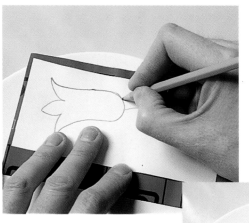

1 *Cut away any excess paper from your drawing. Place a piece of carbon paper betwen the drawing and the ceramic surface. Start to outline around the design, pressing firmly with the stylus or a pencil.*

2 *Lift the edge of the carbon paper to check that the design is being transferred and is positioned correctly. If it isn't, you can remove the transferred design with an eraser and start again. If the lines are incomplete, press harder with the stylus. Finish tracing around the design.*

3 *Remove the sketch and carbon paper to reveal the design—you can now select your color and begin to paint. Designs can be applied straight onto the ceramic surface or on top of a base color. If using a base color, make sure it is completely dry or the pressure of the stylus may dig into the surface and leave an unwanted mark.*

TECHNIQUES

ON THE FOLLOWING *pages we have described a number of painting techniques that you will need to master before you begin painting. If you are a beginner, make sure that you practice the technique required to do your chosen design until you feel confident before starting on your ceramic piece.*

GENERAL TIPS

It is always a good idea to draw your design on a piece of paper before starting on the object, particularly if you are a beginner. This will allow you to figure out the various stages of the design, and the order in which you should apply the colors.

If you are a beginner you might find it easier to try the simple designs that require only a few colors before tackling the more complex designs.

Always ensure that the surface you are going to decorate is clean and free from grease—if in doubt give it a wipe with a tissue or soft cloth dipped in methylated spirit, then let it dry for a minute.

If you have any cutting out to do, there are a few things to keep in mind. Always use a sharp scalpel or craft knife and always use a metal ruler to cut straight edges. It is best to cut onto a cutting mat or other suitable surface. Try and use a flowing motion when you are cutting—if you stop and start, you will not have a clean line on the edge of the mask or stencil. Be patient when cutting—it is safer and results in better work.

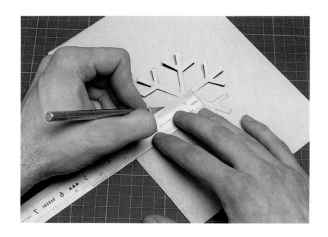

▶ *It is easier and safer to use a cutting mat when preparing your templates. Always use a slow, smooth stroke when cutting, and make sure your knife or scalpel has a sharp blade to ensure a clean cut.*

① *When painting, use slow, steady strokes to ensure a smooth line. Make sure your ceramic is held firmly so that it doesn't slip.*

② *Always wait for the paint to dry before working in the same area with another color—it can be difficult to disguise a smudge.*

③ *Do not worry if your lines are a little wobbly; this adds to the design and hand-painted feel. Remember to rinse your brush thoroughly when changing colors—a bright, sunny yellow will become a dirty green if you have any vestiges of blue on your brush.*

MASKING

Masking is the technique used when you cover part of the surface of an object prior to painting. This can be done with film, tape, or a liquid mask. The area covered by the mask will then remain blank after the mask is removed.

This technique is particularly effective for creating crisp, clean edges and allows you to paint more freely without worrying about staying within the lines of your design. This page and the following one give more detail about all three techniques.

MASKING LIQUID

This is usually a latex-based substance and when dry it has a certain elasticity. You treat it like paint and apply it with a brush. This liquid allows for the masking of detailed areas. However, with this method the ceramic paint must be thoroughly dry before the mask can be removed. Just slip the point of the scalpel under the mask and ease it gently away from the ceramic surface.

1 *Sketch or trace your design onto the ceramic item using a graphite pencil. Apply one good coat of latex over the entire design, making sure that you leave no gaps within the shape which you want to be masked off.*

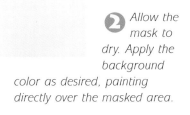

2 *Allow the mask to dry. Apply the background color as desired, painting directly over the masked area.*

3 *The mask can be removed once the background color has lost its shiny, wet look. Slide the tip of your scalpel under one edge of the mask and carefully lift it up.*

4 *Pull the mask back over itself. It will come away in one piece leaving a clean area for applying your design.*

MASKING FILM OR PAPER

This is usually sold in rolls as a clear film with a sticky surface. You can mark up the area to be masked by drawing it onto the backing paper, but remember that it will be in reverse. Alternatively, put your design on tracing paper, stick it to the masking film, and cut around the traced design.

Having cut out your design, peel off the backing paper and stick the film to your object, getting rid of any air bubbles. Make sure that it is firmly stuck at the edges to prevent any paint from seeping underneath. Apply the paint to the surface, and once the paint has started to dry, carefully peel the film away. If any paint does seep under the film, you can carefully scrape it away with a scalpel blade, or use a dampened cotton swab or a tissue to clean up the edge.

MASKING TAPE

This is particularly good for creating a hard, sharp edge. Having figured out the area you want masked, make sure that the surface is grease free and stick the strips of tape to the ceramic piece. Paint along the lines of the tape to reduce the risk of paint seeping under the edges of the tape.

PAINTING

Painting is an activity which nearly everyone has experienced, even if it was long ago at school. It is very versatile, and when it comes to ceramic decoration it allows us great flexibility in executing our designs, from the most delicate of brush strokes to the application of broad swathes of color.

Always shake the bottles of paint well before you use them, so that the paint is well mixed. Ceramic paints might appear slightly thicker than you had anticipated but they can be thinned with either turpentine or water, depending on the type of paint you are using. It is advisable to test the consistency of the paint before you start applying it to your piece of ceramic. Use an old, glazed plate as a test surface. You don't want the paint to be too thin because it will run, spoiling the design; if it is too thick it won't dry properly and will chip too easily.

It is important to use the right brush for the area to be decorated. For instance, if you have a large area with a free, sweeping design, it is best to use a broad or large brush. However, if you are doing a particularly intricate and delicate design then choose a fine brush. Whatever the design you are copying or the brush size you are using, try and keep the brush strokes moving in the same direction. Brush marks can be very apparent on shiny, glazed surfaces.

Paint one color at a time and wait for it to dry completely before you apply another color, otherwise the two colors

may blend. All the paint must be dry before you bake the object in the oven; if you are impatient, a hairdryer will speed the drying process!

You might find it useful to keep a palette of oven-dried colors as a ready reference, showing the final full depth and vividness of each color.

Once the pieces have been baked in the oven and allowed to cool, you can test if the paint is properly dry by carefully scratching the surface with your fingernail. If the paint is completely dry the scratch won't show. Respect the manufacturer's recommended baking temperatures and also the recommended time your ceramic pieces should take to bake. If the baking time is reduced, the process will not work, and if the baking time is increased the colors will tend to brown.

1 *Fan Brush (left)*
This is ideal for covering large areas or backgrounds. It can hold a fair amount of color and gives an even distribution. This is the best style of brush both for creating a watercolor-effect background and for applying repeated coats for a solid, even coverage.

Large, Flat Brush

2 *Large, Flat Brush*

This is a good brush for covering a large area or for bold stripes and line work. Finer, diagonal lines can be produced with the brush held at a 45-degree angle.

3 *Medium, Flat Brush*

This brush is good for smaller areas of solid color or for graded effects. Used sideways, it can produce a bold line, as it will apply more color in a single stroke than a thinner, round brush.

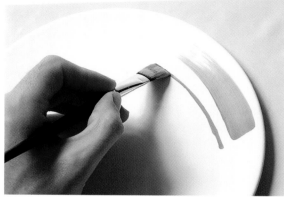

4 *Large, Round Brush*

This brush is essential for the beginner, as it is ideal for a variety of brush strokes. A range of different effects and qualities of line can be achieved by raising and lowering the pressure of the brush.

5 *Medium, Round Brush*

Useful for making petal, leaf, and floral shapes, this brush requires different amounts of pressure during each stroke. The angle of the brush against the ceramic piece will change the thickness of the line.

6 *Fine, Round Brush*

Perfect for fine detail and gentle outlines, this brush is also wonderful for touching in color on large areas or where a mask or stencil has left a gap. It can produce great lines for leaf and petal shapes.

7 *Sponge Stick*

This is the ideal tool for putting a finishing line of color on the outside edge of a piece of work. It can also be used for banded lines or solid areas of color.

STENCILING

Stenciling is a relatively quick and straightforward method of decorating ceramics and is used in conjunction with other decorating techniques such as painting, sponging, and spattering.

A stencil can be cut from stiff watercolor paper if you only intend to use it a few times. If you will be using it repeatedly, it is best to cut it from stencil cardboard, which is more durable.

To make a stencil, first transfer your design onto the cardboard, using the method described in Transferring the Design (see page 13). Then place the cardboard on a cutting mat, hold it down firmly, and start cutting with a scalpel. Try and remember to cut away from your body—rotating the cardboard while you cut helps you to do this. Cut the stencil slightly larger than the design. Your cutting movements should form a smooth, continuous action so that the stencil edge doesn't end up uneven or jagged.

Now that your stencil is cut, stick it to the ceramic surface with masking tape and apply the paint technique of your choice. Two effective paint techniques to use in conjunction with stenciling are sponging and spattering, as they both give a good variation of texture. You might find you need to paint, sponge, or spatter over the edge of the stenciled motif—this makes the outline really sharp.

When you cut a stencil you get two for the price of one; there is the shape you wanted, and there is also its negative. Although initially you may only want to use one, it is a good idea to keep the other one for later projects.

① *Trace or draw the outline of your design onto the stencil material. In this case we are using a leaf shape. Cut out the leaf using a sharp craft knife or scalpel. Always cut toward you, holding the stencil with your free hand but keeping your hand out of the way of the knife. To change direction, turn the stencil, not the knife.*

② *Pour a small amount of underglaze color onto a tile. Pick up a clean, slightly moist sponge and dab one end into the color. Do not push too hard or the color will soak up into the body of the sponge. Dab the sponge about four times in the pool, to distribute the color evenly over the working area of the sponge.*

③ *Place the stencil in the desired location, holding it down firmly. Sponge the color through the cut-out "windows" onto the ceramic surface. Watch out for color running under the edge of the template. Apply as many coats as necessary to achieve the desired density of color.*

④ *Carefully remove the template to reveal the neatly formed leaf. For a variegated leaf, try using two colors. Stenciling leaves of different colors all over the surface of an item would produce a magnificent fall design.*

HOW TO CUT YOUR OWN STENCIL

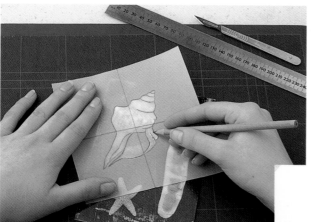

1 Place a sheet of tracing paper over your chosen image and accurately trace as much detail as possible.

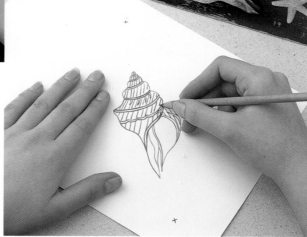

2 Retrace your image onto a piece of thin paper (not shown), pressing hard to leave an imprint. It helps to put something soft underneath the paper, like a magazine. Remove the tracing paper and retrace the lines of the imprint on the paper (left).

3 Divide your drawing into positive and negative parts. The positive parts are the areas that will be painted. Cut out the positive (not shown). Place your design on top of your stencil card. Shade in the areas to be cut out. (see above).

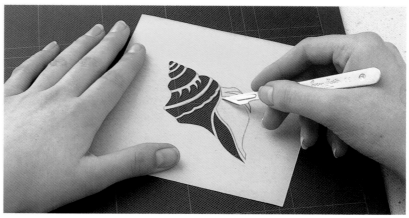

4 Remove the drawing and, using a sharp craft blade, cut around the shaded areas on the card. Rotate your stencil as you work so your cutting action is always in the same direction.

5 Fix your stencil in place with some tape to stop it from slipping. Using a small piece of sponge, dab on the paint. After painting, remove the stencil directly away from the surface to avoid smudging.

SPONGING

Sponging is a great way to cover large areas quickly while at the same time creating an interesting, blotchy texture. It is a method which works well either by itself or in conjunction with stenciling or masking. It is also effective if you decide to use one color on top of another.

For this technique you can use a real sponge, a synthetic sponge, or a scrunched-up cloth or tissue. The finished textures will vary depending on how porous the sponge is, or how tightly the cloth or tissue is scrunched up.

① Select a color to be your base coat and pour a little of the paint onto a plate. Dampen your sponge and cover the whole bowl with the paint, trying to leave as little white showing as possible. Let it dry.

② Select a second color—this should be a glaze —and pour a little of the paint onto a plate as before. Randomly cover the bowl, allowing the first color to show through. Let it dry until it is tacky.

③ Select a second glaze that is paler than the first glaze. Apply it over top of the first glaze, blending it in so the resulting color becomes muted and fuses together. Let it dry completely for twenty-four hours, then varnish with polyurethane varnish.

SPATTERING

Spattering is the technique where you get to use that old toothbrush mentioned in the Materials and Equipment section. It can be fairly messy, so make sure you have plenty of newspaper or other protective covering on your work surface, walls, and floor—and, of course, on yourself!

Rather like sponging, this method creates an interesting texture. Simply dip the old brush into the paint, point it toward your object, and just run your finger down the bristle so the paint spatters across the surface of the ceramic object.

Again, like sponging, spattering looks effective when you use more than one color, or when you spatter with different types and sizes of brushes to get different effects. It can also be used in conjuction with masking and stenciling.

① Spattering can create interesting effects, but make sure you protect the surrounding area, as it can be quite a messy technique!

STAMPING

Decorating ceramics using sponges or stamps is a quick, fun way to apply simple designs. Sponging is not used to produce an accurate result but more to give the decorator a background to work on. Sponge shapes work well on curved surfaces as they will bend to follow the surface contour. Bold, simple shapes are the most suitable for sponges, while stamps can be used for more detailed shapes. Ready-cut sponges and a variety of stamps are available from many specialist suppliers, or you can cut your own from sponge sanding blocks, which will give you an unlimited choice of shapes.

SPONGE STAMPS

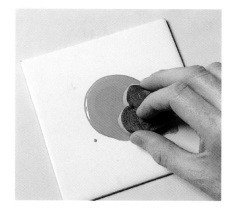

1 *Place a pool of paint on a plate. Gently press the sponge shape into the pool and work it up and down to allow the color to be evenly distributed across the working surface. Avoid pressing too hard as this will force the color up into the body of the sponge, reducing the amount that can be transferred to the ceramic surface.*

2 *Position the sponge above the ceramic piece, then gently push it down onto the surface. Make sure the entire working surface of the sponge comes into contact with the ceramic piece. If the surface is not flat, place one side of the loaded sponge on the surface and gently roll the sponge around the shape.*

3 *Remove the sponge to reveal the transferred design. Repeat the process for further motifs. Any irregularities can be touched up with a smaller piece of sponge to maintain the mottled look.*

RUBBER STAMPS

1 *Place the stamp face down in a pool of paint on a plate. Move the stamp in a circular motion, spreading the color evenly across the plate and allowing the stamp to touch the surface as you do so. Remove any excess paint which may be trapped between any cut-outs with a brush.*

2 *Apply the stamp to the surface to be decorated. Hold for a few seconds to allow the moisture to be absorbed and the color to transfer across. Be sure not to move the stamp sideways or you will smudge the design.*

3 *Remove the stamp. The color image has now been transferred to the ceramic surface. For additional images, place the stamp back in the pool of color and repeat the process. Add more color to the plate if needed.*

SGRAFFITO

Sgraffito is a technique based on incising (scratching) through the painted colors into the surface of an item. Fine detail is easily achieved with either a stylus or a sgraffito tool, while larger areas can be scraped away using the sgraffito tool. The cleared areas can then be left as they are, with the ceramic showing, or filled in with a color. The key to successful sgraffito work is to incise into the color while it is still a little damp. The tool will cut through it, leaving a neat, smooth line.

1 *Apply the base color. Sgraffito works best through dark colors like black or dark blue—the bigger the contrast between the ceramic color and the underglaze, the bolder the finished design will look.*

2 *It is possible to draw or trace your design onto the underglaze with a graphite pencil. Use the stylus to incise around the design. Brush away flakes with a soft brush. If the underglaze is chipping, use a damp sponge to moisten the area.*

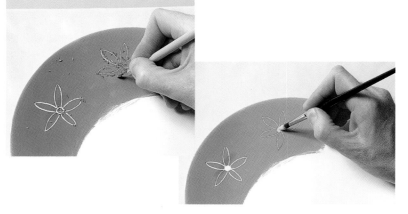

3 *Continue until you have cut out all the outlines and any wider areas, such as the center of the flower. Any color can now be applied directly.*

DOTWORK

Dotwork is an easy way to create a colorful pattern. The instrument you choose is optional. The wrong end of your paint brush is perhaps the handiest. Whatever the implement, the technique of simply dipping it into paint and stamping it onto a surface provides scope for endless creations.

1 *Dip the wooden end of a brush into your chosen color of paint. One dip will make a succession of approximately five or six graduated dots. Apply the dots in an arch.*

2 *Continue on with as many colors as you like in the same manner.*

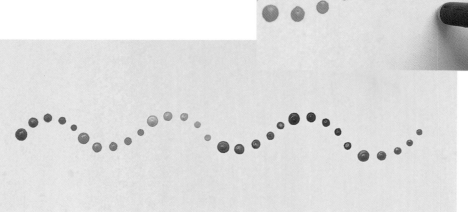

3 *This attractive dotwork rainbow border could be continued to any length and used effectively in a multitude of ceramic designs.*

DESIGNS IN COLOR

BEING CREATIVE WITH *color is one of the most challenging and effective aspects of ceramic design. It is well worth learning a little about the "science of color" to maximize the impact of your work. Use the color wheel (see below) to plan your own color schemes—you don't have to follow those shown in the templates!*

THE COLOR WHEEL

The color wheel is based around the three primary colors (red, yellow, and blue), interspersed with the three secondary colors (orange, green, and purple). Each secondary color is formed by combining the two primary colors that are adjacent to it on the wheel.

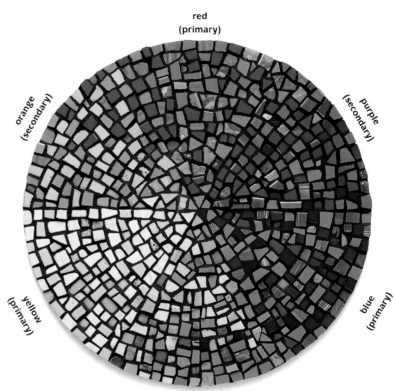

red
(primary)

orange
(secondary)

purple
(secondary)

yellow
(primary)

blue
(primary)

green
(secondary)

Complementary colors
Complementary colors are those which lie directly opposite each other on the color wheel. You can give a design more impact by using complementary colors together, as in this tile, where the turquoise complementary has been used to liven up the orange.

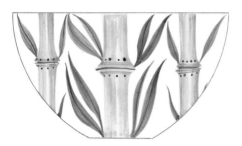

Similar tones
You don't have to use a contrasting color to make a design work. Here the design uses a selection of colors from a similar area of the color wheel to create a calm, relaxing effect.

Varied tones
Here there is no limit to the palette used. The variety of tones used creates a bright, vibrant design—a carnival of colors.

Cool colors
Cool colors are those which reflect mainly blue light. You will find that blues, turquoises, and greens give a cool, fresh, restful appearance to a design.

Warm colors
Warm colors reflect mainly red light. A design which uses reds, oranges, and yellows will have a warm, energetic, lively feel.

ROUNDED CUP & SAUCER 1

THIS CLASSIC *cup-and-saucer shape has endless design possibilities, from the simple graduated dots of Design 1 to the lush brush strokes of the rose clusters in Design 7. The alphabet used in Design 2 is only an introduction to the many uses of letters as design motifs. The grapes and vine leaves of Design 5 have a traditional appeal, in contrast to the modern geometric lines of Design 6 which require extra care in masking prior to painting. The sailboat design combines the techniques of stenciling and painting lines, while the gift box pattern of Design 8 is only slightly more challenging.*

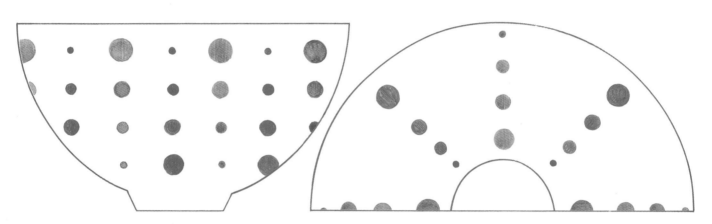

1

COLORS ● ● **TECHNIQUE:** *Painting*

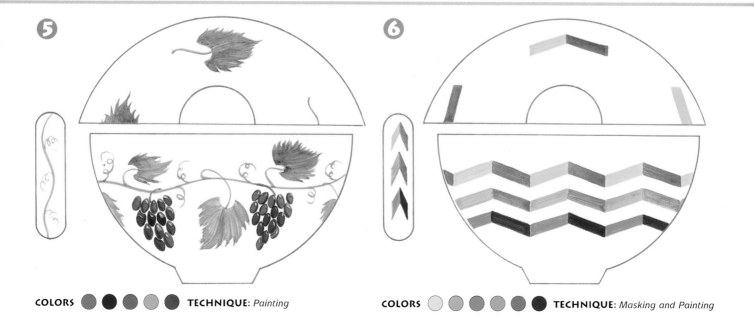

5

COLORS ● ● ● ● ● **TECHNIQUE:** *Painting*

6

COLORS ● ● ● ● ● ● **TECHNIQUE:** *Masking and Painting*

COLORS ⚪🔵🔵🔵🔵🔵🔵🔵⚫🔵 **TECHNIQUE:** *Painting*

COLORS
🔴🔴🔴
TECHNIQUE:
Stenciling and Painting

COLORS
🔵🔵⚫🔵
TECHNIQUE:
Stenciling and Painting

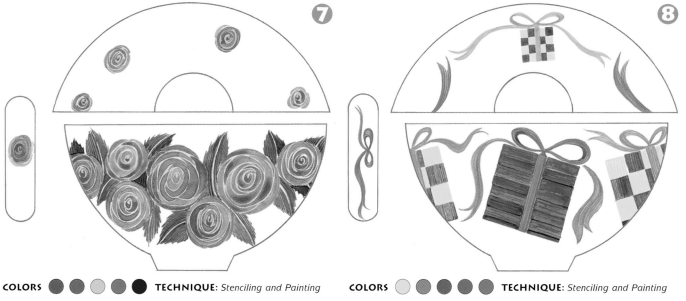

COLORS 🔵🔵⚪🔵⚫ **TECHNIQUE:** *Stenciling and Painting*

COLORS ⚪🔵🔵🔵🔵 **TECHNIQUE:** *Stenciling and Painting*

25

ROUNDED **CUP & SAUCER 2**

THE SIMPLICITY OF *the banding combined with the shaded blue dots in Design 1 gives confidence to the beginner. Design 2 has just a hint of the Christmas season about it, while the bold colors and shapes used in Design 3 give this classic cup a modern look. You can paint on a few bar lines from your favorite song for a unique touch with Design 4. The acorns and oak leaves of Design 5 and the pansies of Design 6 show what an endless resource nature is for design ideas, as do the more traditional nature themes in Designs 7 and 8.*

❶

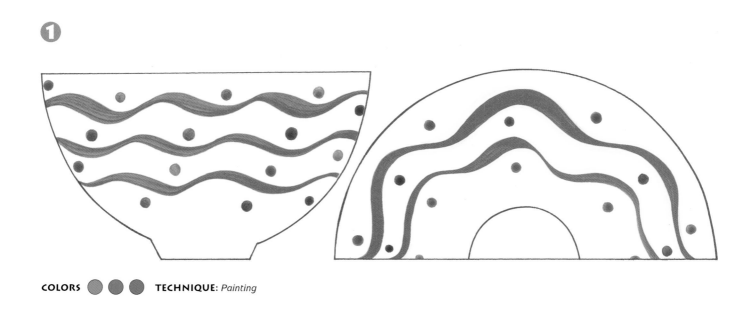

COLORS ⚫⚫⚫ **TECHNIQUE:** *Painting*

❺

❻

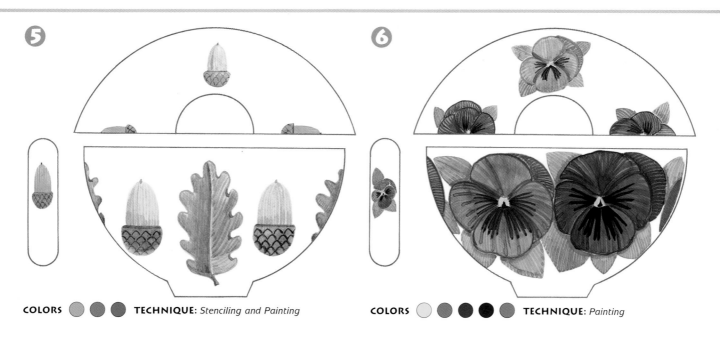

COLORS ⚫⚫⚫ **TECHNIQUE:** *Stenciling and Painting*

COLORS ⚫⚫⚫⚫⚫ **TECHNIQUE:** *Painting*

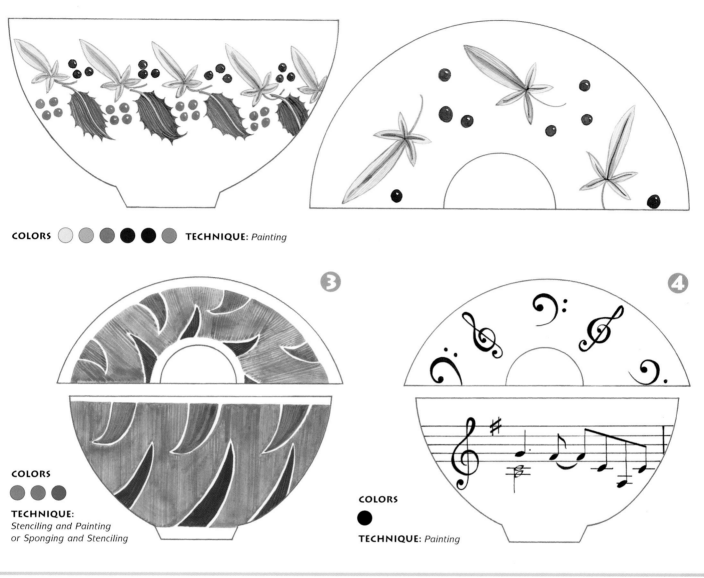

COLORS ⚪ 🔵 🔵 ⚫ ⚫ 🔵 **TECHNIQUE:** *Painting*

③

COLORS
🔵 🔵 🔵

TECHNIQUE:
*Stenciling and Painting
or Sponging and Stenciling*

④

COLORS
⚫

TECHNIQUE: *Painting*

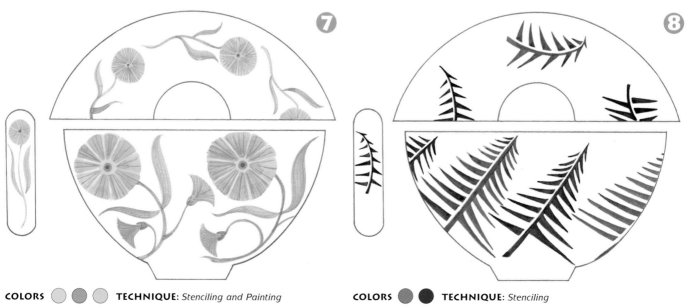

COLORS ⚪ 🔵 ⚪ **TECHNIQUE:** *Stenciling and Painting*

COLORS 🔵 ⚫ **TECHNIQUE:** *Stenciling*

27

STRAIGHT-SIDED **CUP & SAUCER**

HERE IS ANOTHER *popular cup-and-saucer shape, but with a slightly larger canvas for your designs. The lemon slices and dark leaves of Design 1 can be applied by painting or stenciling techniques; the same goes for the tulips and the geometric patterns shown in Designs 5 and 6. The moons and stars in Design 2 require a combination of painting and stenciling. As with letters, any use of numbers in a design requires a steady hand, and Design 3 is no exception. The flowers in Designs 4 and 7 could be applied using a combination of sponging and stenciling techniques. Astrological images, such as the Cancerian crab shown in Design 8, are another popular design idea.*

❶

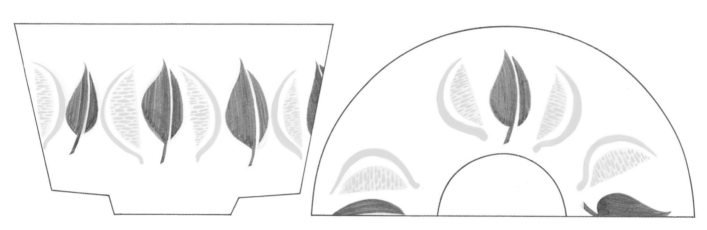

COLORS ⚪⚫ **TECHNIQUE:** *Stenciling*

❺ 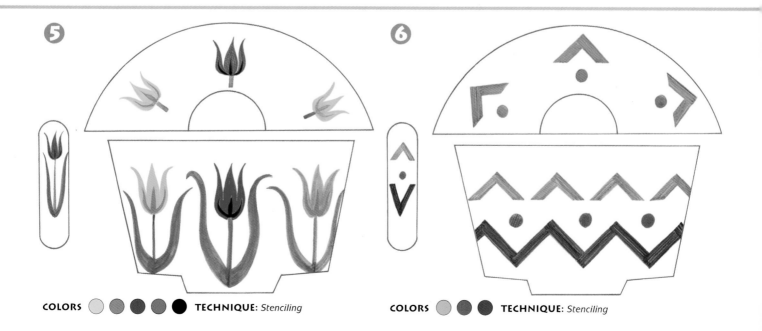 **❻**

COLORS ⚪⚫⚫⚫⚫ **TECHNIQUE:** *Stenciling*   COLORS ⚪⚫⚫ **TECHNIQUE:** *Stenciling*

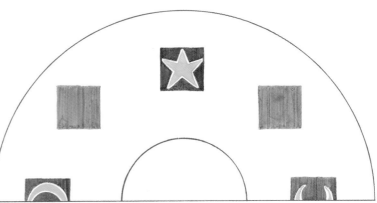

COLORS ● ● ● ● **TECHNIQUE:** *Stenciling, Painting, and Masking*

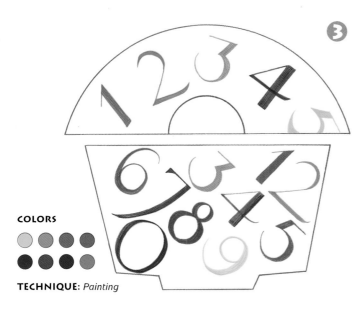

COLORS
● ● ● ●
● ● ● ●

TECHNIQUE: *Painting*

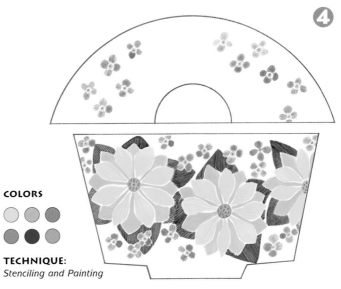

COLORS
● ● ●
● ● ●

TECHNIQUE:
Stenciling and Painting

COLORS ● ● ● ● ● ● **TECHNIQUE:** *Stenciling and Painting*

COLORS ● ● ● **TECHNIQUE:** *Stenciling, Painting, and Sponging*

STRAIGHT-SIDED **MUG**

THE STRAIGHT SIDES *of this mug create a flat "canvas" that is easy to paint. Design 1 shows a traditional tartan pattern but uses non-traditional color combinations to give the design more flair. In Design 2, notice how fruit shapes look more effective if you keep your brush strokes moving in the same direction. Simple, bold designs such as painted or stenciled hearts and geometric patterns are an easy way in beginners. The seahorses require a more experienced hand. Themed designs, such as a sailboat anchor or a farmer's weather vane, could reflect some aspect of your home decoration.*

❶

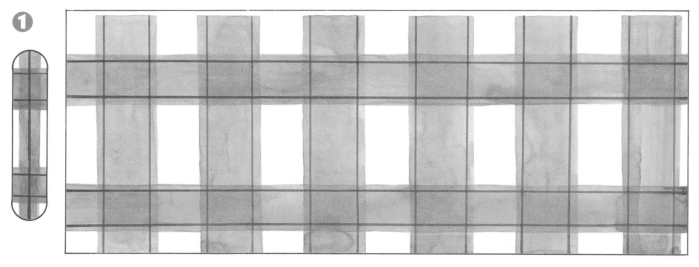

COLORS ● ● ● **TECHNIQUE:** *Painting*

❺

COLORS ○ ○ ● ● ● **TECHNIQUE:** *Stenciling and Painting*

❻

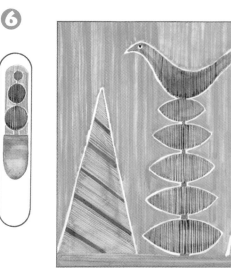

COLORS ● ● ● ● **TECHNIQUE:** *Stenciling and Painting*

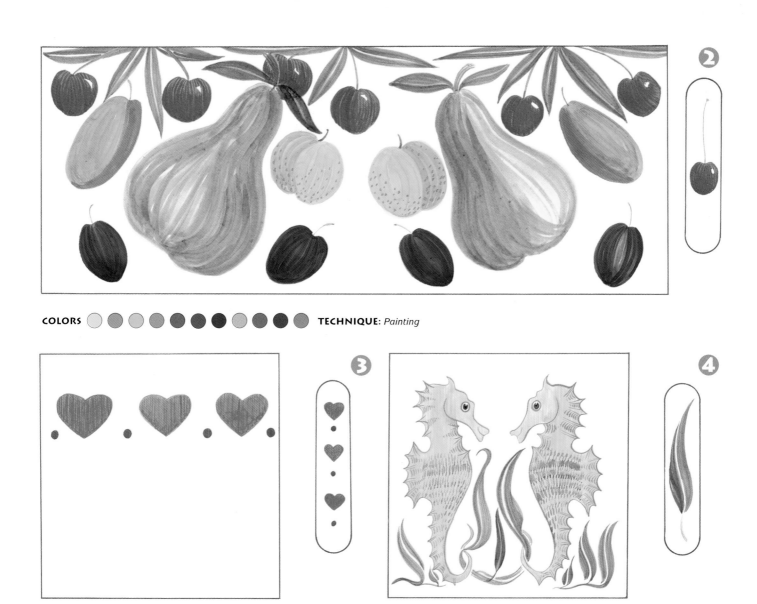

2

COLORS ⚪⚫⚫⚫⚫⚫⚫⚫⚫⚫⚫ **TECHNIQUE:** *Painting*

3

COLORS ⚫⚫ **TECHNIQUE:** *Stenciling*

4

COLORS ⚪⚪⚫⚫⚫ **TECHNIQUE:** *Stenciling and Painting*

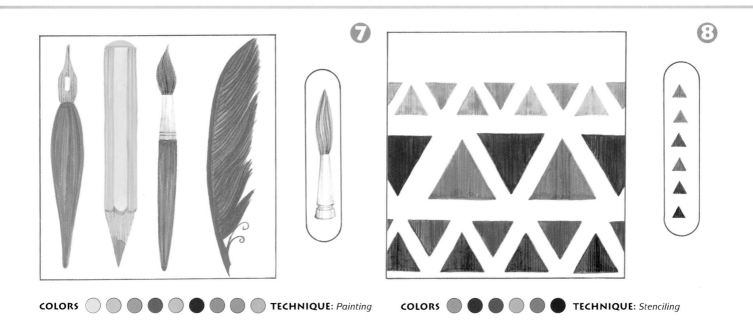

7

COLORS ⚪⚫⚫⚫⚫⚫⚫⚫⚪ **TECHNIQUE:** *Painting*

8

COLORS ⚫⚫⚫⚫⚪⚫⚫ **TECHNIQUE:** *Stenciling*

CURVED **MUG**

THE SWOLLEN BASE *of this type of mug provides an interesting shape for a variety of designs. The simple repeat pattern of Design 1 can be either stenciled or painted. The abstract look of Design 5 shows that white spaces, here forming star shapes, are often as important as the painted area in the overall design; the white spaces around the peas and pods of design 8 are also very striking. Notice how curved and wavy lines accentuate the rounded shape of this mug. If you extend your designs to the mug handle, you will achieve this effect in full.*

COLORS ⬤⬤⬤ **TECHNIQUE:** *Stenciling or Painting*

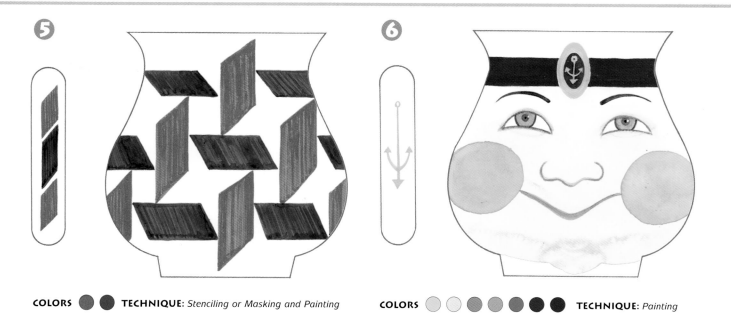

COLORS ⬤⬤ **TECHNIQUE:** *Stenciling or Masking and Painting*

COLORS ⬤⬤⬤⬤⬤⬤⬤ **TECHNIQUE:** *Painting*

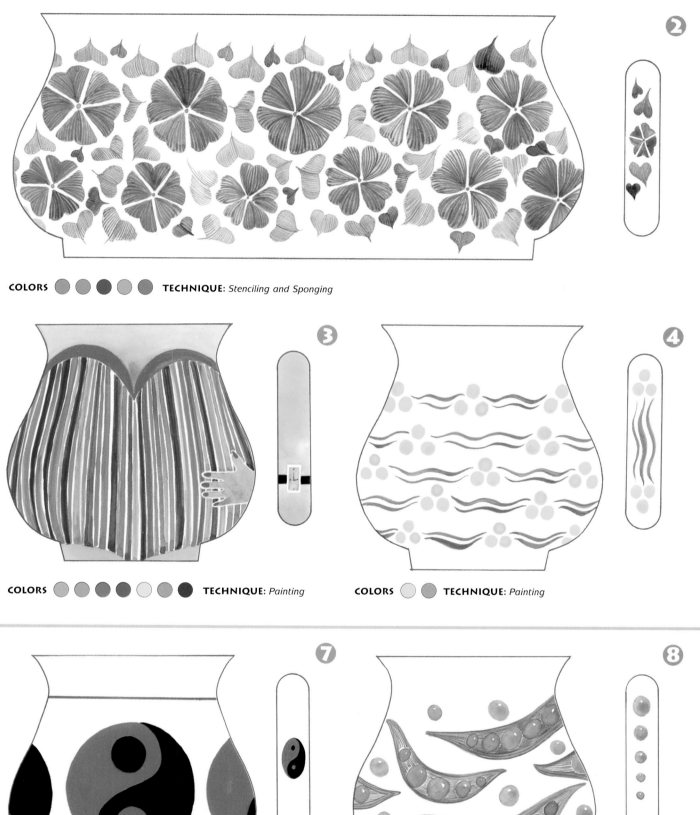

COLORS ⬤ ⬤ ⬤ ⬤ ⬤ **TECHNIQUE:** *Stenciling and Sponging*

COLORS ⬤ ⬤ ⬤ ⬤ ⬤ ⬤ ⬤ **TECHNIQUE:** *Painting*

COLORS ⬤ ⬤ **TECHNIQUE:** *Painting*

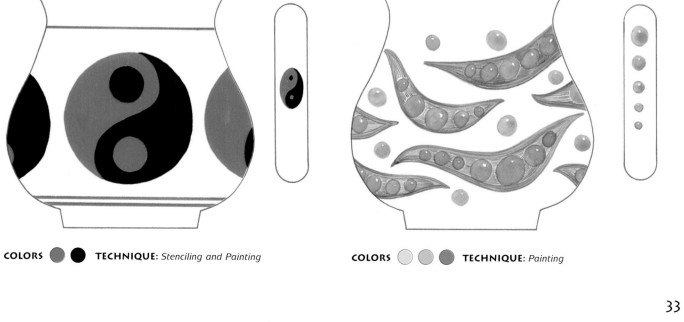

COLORS ⬤ ⬤ **TECHNIQUE:** *Stenciling and Painting*

COLORS ⬤ ⬤ ⬤ **TECHNIQUE:** *Painting*

CONE **MUG**

NOTICE HOW SOME *of the designs for this mug echo its overall shape, albeit sometimes in reverse. Design 1 uses "The Green Man", a familiar figure in European folklore who has his equivalents in many other cultures. To achieve the sunrise effect of Design 2, you need to apply careful masking before you start painting. See how the poppies of Design 3 are enhanced by the areas left white. Allow yourself the freedom of spontaneity and personal flair when painting the zigzag lines of Design 8—sometimes perfection can be boring!*

❶

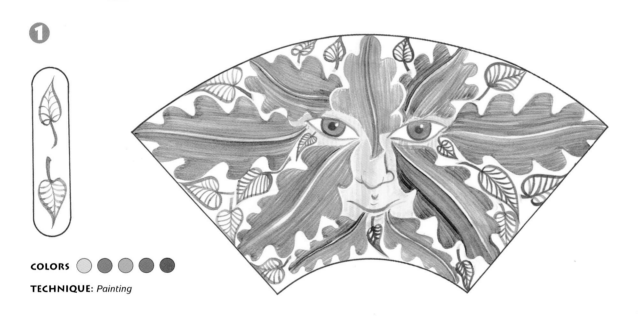

COLORS ● ● ● ● ●

TECHNIQUE: *Painting*

❺

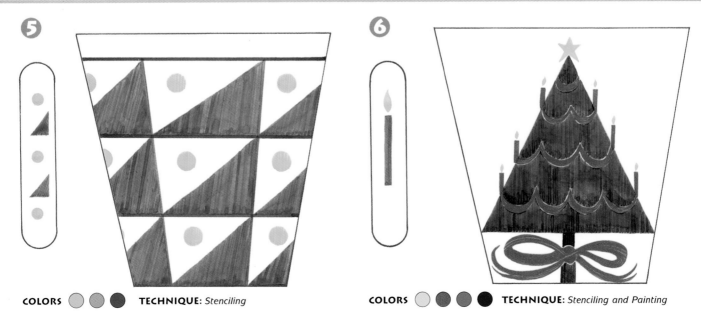

COLORS ● ● ●   **TECHNIQUE:** *Stenciling*

❻

COLORS ● ● ● ●   **TECHNIQUE:** *Stenciling and Painting*

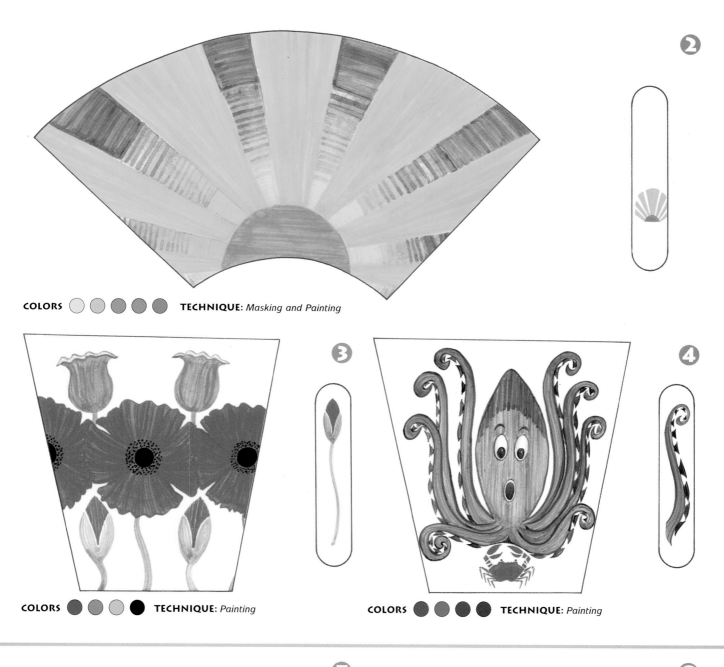

2

COLORS ○ ○ ● ● ●   **TECHNIQUE:** *Masking and Painting*

3

COLORS ● ● ○ ●   **TECHNIQUE:** *Painting*

4

COLORS ● ● ● ●   **TECHNIQUE:** *Painting*

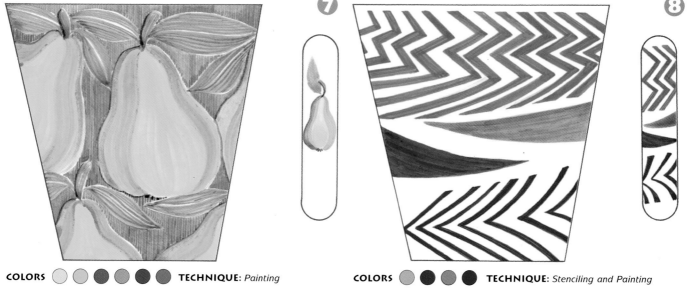

7

COLORS ○ ○ ● ● ● ●   **TECHNIQUE:** *Painting*

8

COLORS ● ● ● ●   **TECHNIQUE:** *Stenciling and Painting*

STRAIGHT-SIDED **BEAKER**

THIS BEAKER SHAPE is often used in bathrooms for holding toothbrushes and tubes of toothpaste. Therefore, you will probably want the design to complement your bathroom decor. Seaside images are very common, as shown here in the lighthouse and fish designs. If you are using stencils to recreate these patterns, as in Designs 3, 7, and 8, why stop at the border? You could also stencil other bathroom fixtures or even the walls, creating an overall design motif.

①

COLORS ●●●● **TECHNIQUE:** Stenciling and Painting

⑤

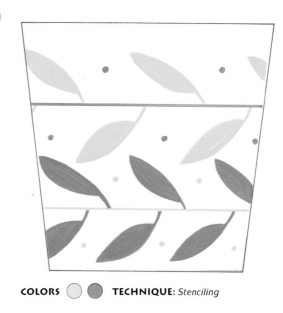

COLORS
●●●●
●●●●

TECHNIQUE:
Stenciling and Painting

⑥

COLORS ○● **TECHNIQUE:** Stenciling

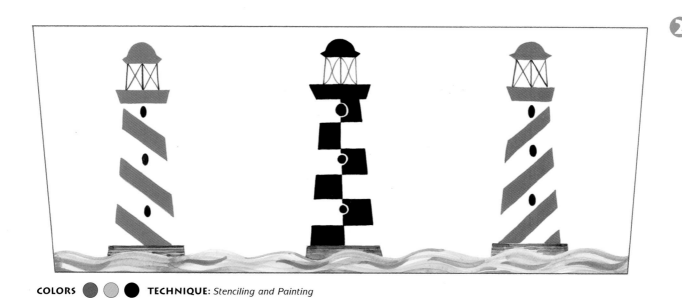

COLORS ● ● ● **TECHNIQUE:** *Stenciling and Painting*

COLORS ● ● ● ● **TECHNIQUE:** *Stenciling*

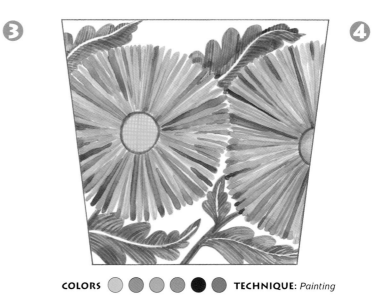

COLORS ○ ● ● ● ● ● ● **TECHNIQUE:** *Painting*

COLORS ● ● ● ● **TECHNIQUE:** *Stenciling*

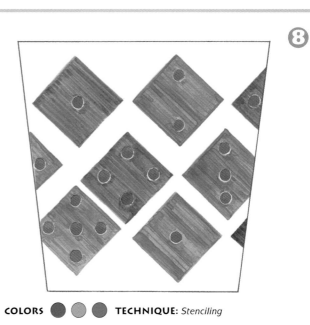

COLORS ● ● ● **TECHNIQUE:** *Stenciling*

ROUND **SUGAR BOWL**

THE DECORATIONS ON *these bowls could also be applied to rounded cups, pitchers, and teapots to create an entire tea set or coffee set. Designs 1, 6, and 9 are simple stencil designs. The abstract patterns of Designs 3 and 7 would work well with a combination of stenciling and painting, as would the cheeky owls of Design 4. The bamboo stalks of Design 2 and the strawberries of Design 8 can be painted freehand, but remember to keep the brush strokes going in the same direction. The filled-in blue-painted background of Design 5 really helps the white snowdrops to stand out.*

1

COLORS ● ● **TECHNIQUE:** *Stenciling*

6

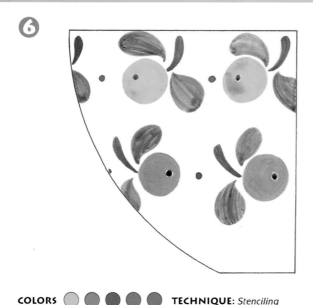

COLORS ○ ● ● ● ● **TECHNIQUE:** *Stenciling*

7

COLORS ○ ● ● **TECHNIQUE:** *Stenciling and Painting*

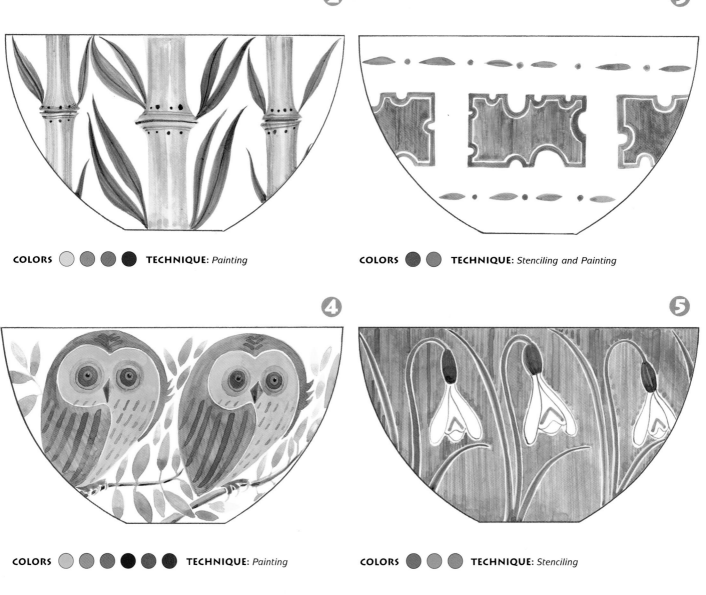

2

COLORS ● ● ● ● **TECHNIQUE:** *Painting*

3

COLORS ● ● **TECHNIQUE:** *Stenciling and Painting*

4

COLORS ● ● ● ● ● ● **TECHNIQUE:** *Painting*

5

COLORS ● ● ● **TECHNIQUE:** *Stenciling*

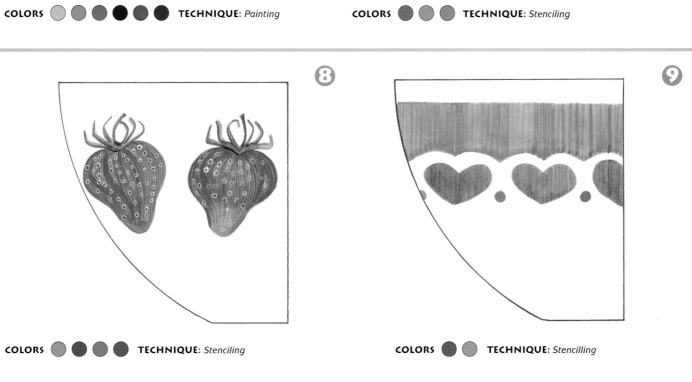

8

COLORS ● ● ● ● **TECHNIQUE:** *Stenciling*

9

COLORS ● ● **TECHNIQUE:** *Stencilling*

LIPPED **BOWL**

THE CIRCULAR SHAPE *of this bowl is ideal for a continuous border design, whether you opt for an abstract or a figurative one. The decorations suggested here are for both the rims and the sides of the bowls. The floral look of Design 1 and the abstract jigsaw style of Design 5 could be done very simply by using a stencil. For the simple floral effect of Design 2 you could easily use a sponging technique over the stencil, to soften its intensity. If you have a firm hand, then the strong lines and triangles of Design 3 could be painted directly onto the bowl.*

1

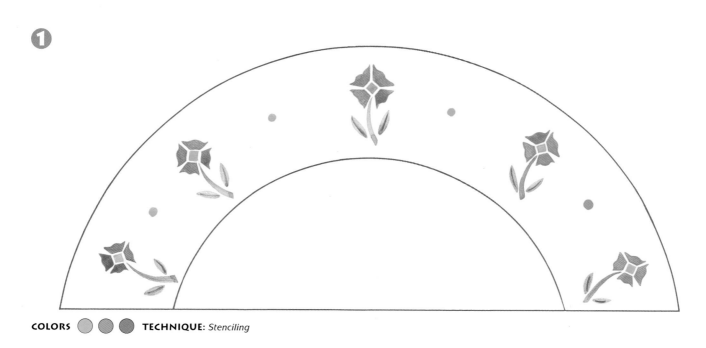

COLORS ⚪ ⚫ ⚫ **TECHNIQUE:** *Stenciling*

5

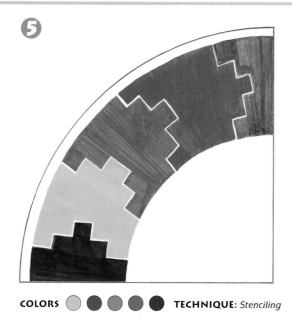

COLORS ⚪ ⚫ ⚫ ⚫ ⚫ **TECHNIQUE:** *Stenciling*

6

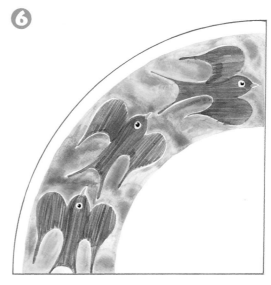

COLORS ⚪ ⚫ ⚫ ⚫ **TECHNIQUE:** *Stenciling and Painting*

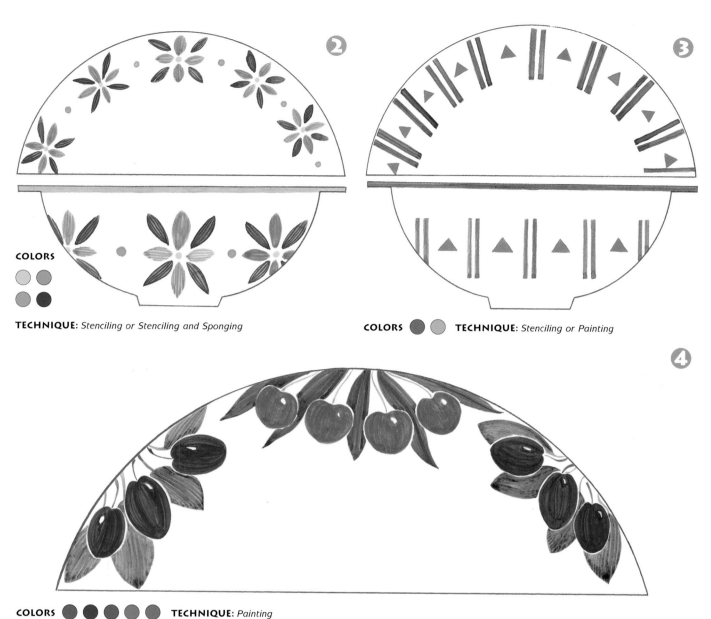

②

COLORS ●● ●●

TECHNIQUE: *Stenciling or Stenciling and Sponging*

③

COLORS ●● **TECHNIQUE:** *Stenciling or Painting*

④

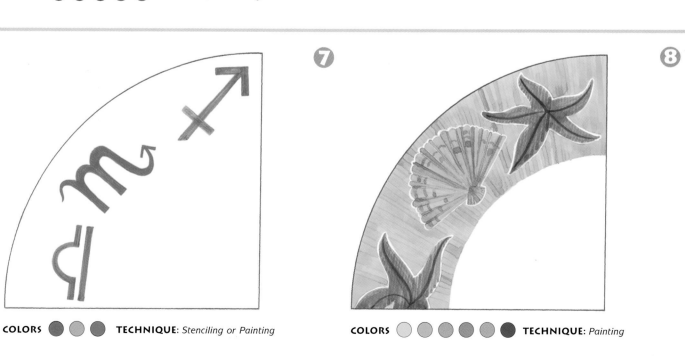

COLORS ●●●●● **TECHNIQUE:** *Painting*

⑦

COLORS ●●● **TECHNIQUE:** *Stenciling or Painting*

⑧

COLORS ●●●●●● **TECHNIQUE:** *Painting*

UNLIPPED **BOWL**

WHEN CHOOSING A decoration for this unlipped bowl, you will find many that go well with the full curves of its shape. Notice how the painted backgrounds of Designs 2, 4, and 5 make these designs really stand out. For beginners, the floral pattern of Design 6 is easy to achieve with the use of a stencil, and the stripes of Design 7 should present no problem if you use a masking technique. The gridlike Design 8 is best achieved by using masking tape. The butterflies of Design 9 can be done by using a stencil and then painting over for the detail.

①

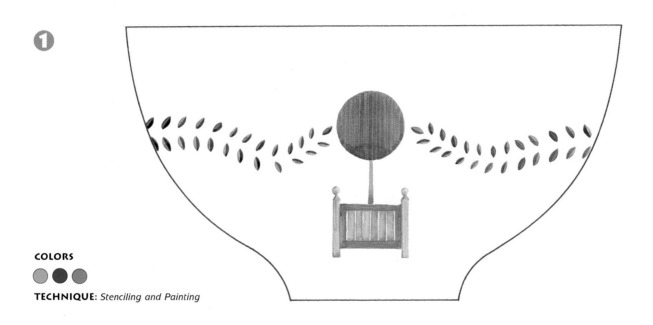

COLORS
● ● ●

TECHNIQUE: *Stenciling and Painting*

⑥

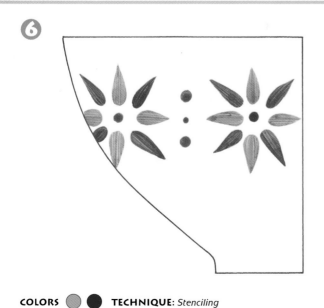

COLORS ● ● **TECHNIQUE:** *Stenciling*

⑦

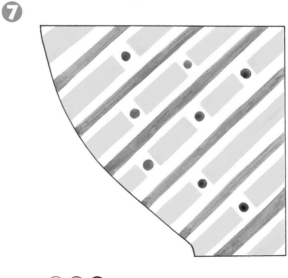

COLORS ● ● ● **TECHNIQUE:** *Masking and Painting*

②

COLORS ⚪ ⚪ ⚪ ⚫ **TECHNIQUE:** *Stenciling and Painting*

③

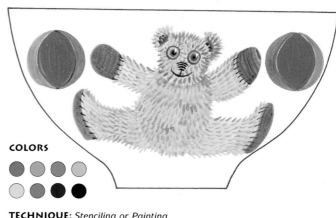

COLORS
⚪ ⚪ ⚪ ⚪
⚪ ⚪ ⚫ ⚫

TECHNIQUE: *Stenciling or Painting*

④

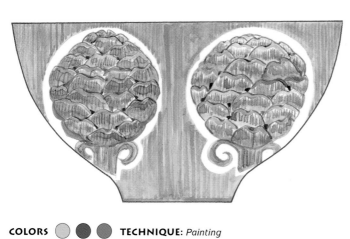

COLORS ⚪ ⚫ ⚫ **TECHNIQUE:** *Painting*

⑤

COLORS
⚪ ⚪ ⚪ ⚫
⚫ ⚪ ⚪ ⚫

TECHNIQUE: *Stenciling or Painting*

⑧

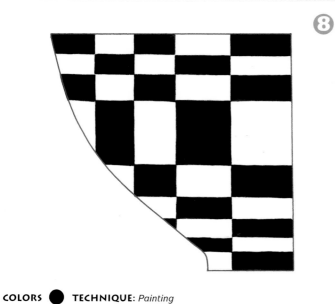

COLORS ⚫ **TECHNIQUE:** *Painting*

⑨

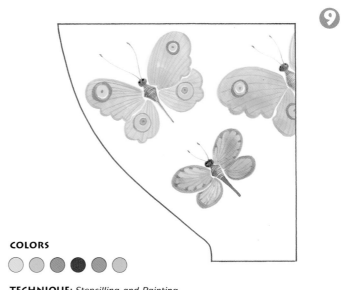

COLORS
⚪ ⚪ ⚪ ⚫ ⚪ ⚪

TECHNIQUE: *Stencilling and Painting*

43

CONE **BOWL**

THIS NICE DEEP *bowl allows plenty of room for imaginative decorating. The Halloween faces of the carved pumpkins in Design 1 look great, and they can be simply achieved by stenciling and then painting over with the detail. The same techniques can be used for the border of radishes in Design 6. When it comes to the abstract swirls of Design 7, however, these are best painted freely with a confident hand; in most cases it is best to practice painting freehand designs on paper before painting them onto your ceramic object. The juggling clown of Design 2 and the Roman numerals of Design 5 need to be marked out carefully before you start painting.*

1

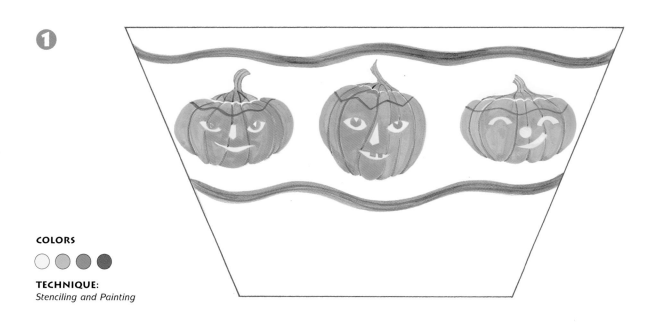

COLORS
○ ○ ● ●

TECHNIQUE:
Stenciling and Painting

6

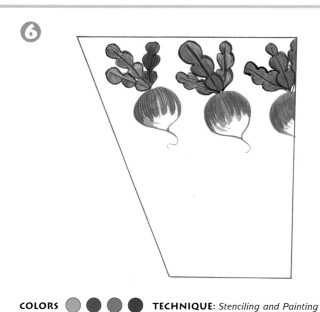

7

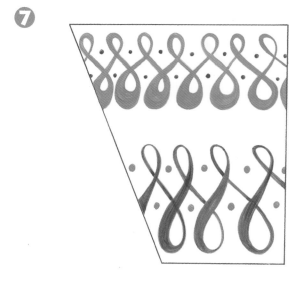

COLORS ● ● ● ● **TECHNIQUE:** *Stenciling and Painting*

COLORS ● ● **TECHNIQUE:** *Painting*

44

2

COLORS

TECHNIQUE: *Masking and Painting*

3

COLORS

TECHNIQUE: *Stenciling and Painting*

4

COLORS **TECHNIQUE:** *Painting*

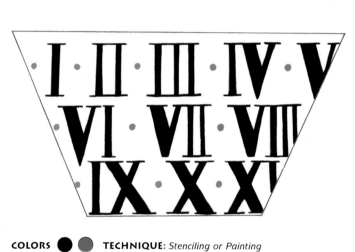

5

COLORS **TECHNIQUE:** *Stenciling or Painting*

8

COLORS

TECHNIQUE: *Stenciling and Painting*

9

COLORS

TECHNIQUE: *Painting*

45

LARGE SALAD/FRUIT **BOWL**

WHEN IT COMES *to choosing a design for these larger pieces, the temptation is to go for big, bold designs. These designs will certainly look wonderful, as is shown by the flowers in Designs 2 and 6, and the fruit in Design 4, but don't forget that smaller, more delicate designs can look just as good when the colors are chosen carefully. The boldly decorated alphabet of Design 1 requires accurate marking up, but then you can paint it fairly freely, while the abstract pattern of Design 3 needs careful masking to achieve those beautiful, crisp lines. The gorgeous animals which leap and swim around the bowl in Designs 5 and 8 can be created by stenciling and then painting over.*

①

COLORS

TECHNIQUE: *Painting*

⑥

⑦

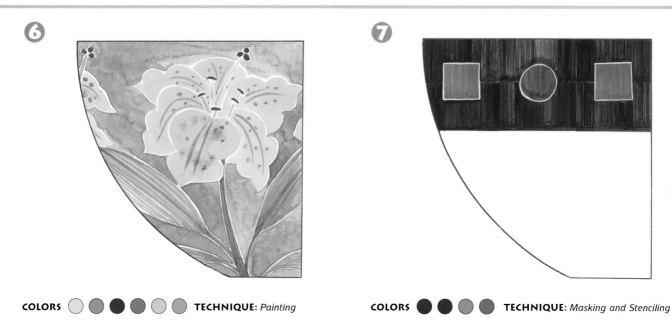

COLORS **TECHNIQUE:** *Painting*   **COLORS** **TECHNIQUE:** *Masking and Stenciling*

46

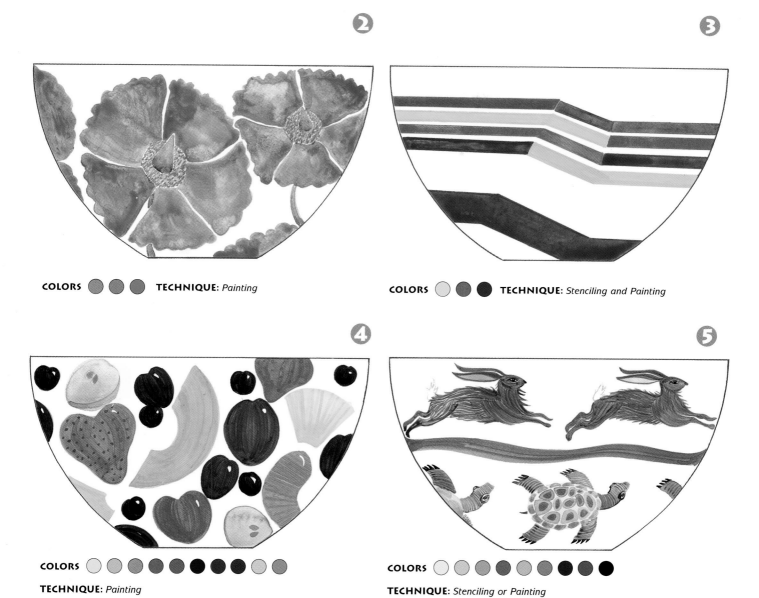

COLORS ⬤⬤⬤ **TECHNIQUE:** *Painting*

COLORS ⬤⬤⬤ **TECHNIQUE:** *Stenciling and Painting*

COLORS ⬤⬤⬤⬤⬤⬤⬤⬤⬤⬤
TECHNIQUE: *Painting*

COLORS ⬤⬤⬤⬤⬤⬤⬤⬤⬤⬤
TECHNIQUE: *Stenciling or Painting*

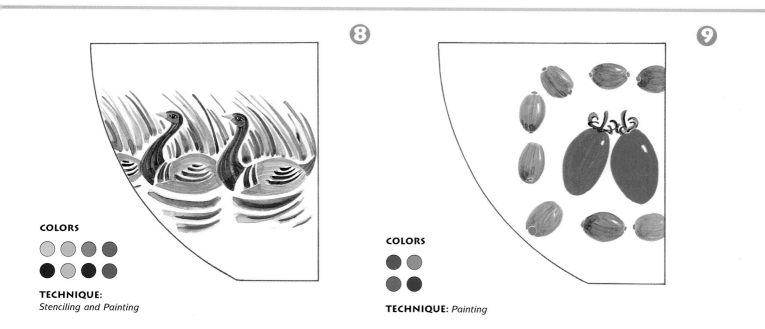

COLORS
⬤⬤⬤⬤
⬤⬤⬤⬤

TECHNIQUE:
Stenciling and Painting

COLORS
⬤⬤
⬤⬤

TECHNIQUE: *Painting*

LARGE, SHALLOW **BOWL**

THIS STYLE OF *bowl is commonly used to serve pasta. The focus of the design is generally at the concave center of the bowl, because the sides are very low and not very visible. Most of the designs on these pages can be reproduced by using a stencil and then painting over with the details. A little care is needed in arranging the glasses in Design 4 before painting; the large, relatively flat "canvas" of a pasta bowl is excellent for these bigger compositions, as is shown here and in Design 3. The wavy abstract lines of Design 6 can be painted freely, then a stencil could be used to create the squares, perhaps with a sponged effect.*

①

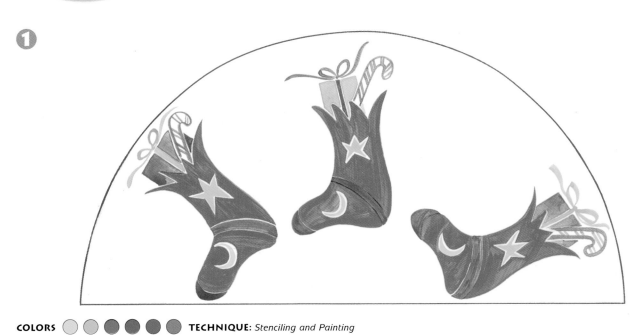

COLORS ⬤⬤⬤⬤⬤⬤ **TECHNIQUE:** *Stenciling and Painting*

⑥

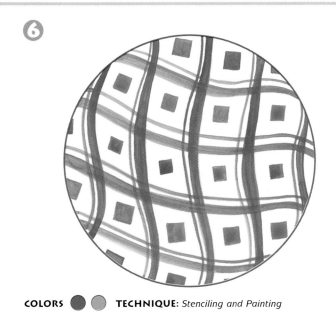

COLORS ⬤⬤ **TECHNIQUE:** *Stenciling and Painting*

⑦

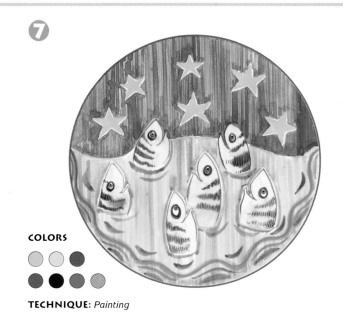

COLORS
⬤⬤⬤
⬤⬤⬤⬤

TECHNIQUE: *Painting*

48

COLORS ⬤⬤⬤⬤⬤   **TECHNIQUE:** *Stenciling and Painting*   **COLORS** ⬤⬤⬤⬤⬤   **TECHNIQUE:** *Painting*

COLORS ⬤⬤⬤⬤⬤⬤⬤⬤⬤   **TECHNIQUE:** *Painting*   **COLORS** ⬤⬤⬤⬤   **TECHNIQUE:** *Stenciling and Painting*

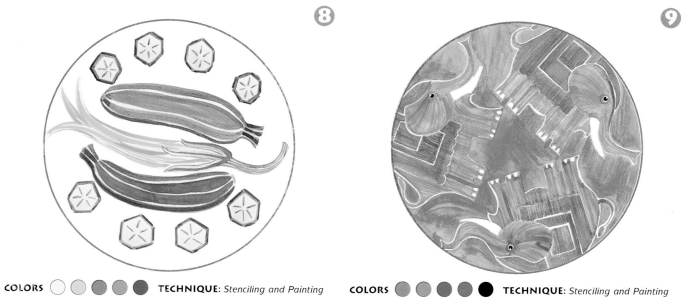

COLORS ⬤⬤⬤⬤⬤   **TECHNIQUE:** *Stenciling and Painting*   **COLORS** ⬤⬤⬤⬤⬤   **TECHNIQUE:** *Stenciling and Painting*

SMALL JUG

AS WITH THE *designs for the assorted cup shapes, there are many patterns that will complement the curvy shape of the pitcher—don't forget to extend your design to the handle to maximize the effect. If Design 2, with its zigzag and floral effect, appeals to you, then you will probably have to combine masking and stenciling techniques. The hearts of Design 3, and the flowers and the buzzing bees of Design 5, can be created by using a stencil and then painting over with the detail. The simple wavy lines of Design 6 and the fruit in Design 8 can be painted freehand.*

1

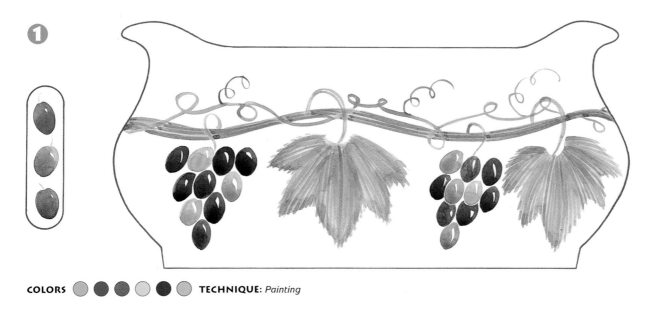

COLORS ● ● ● ● ● ● **TECHNIQUE:** *Painting*

5

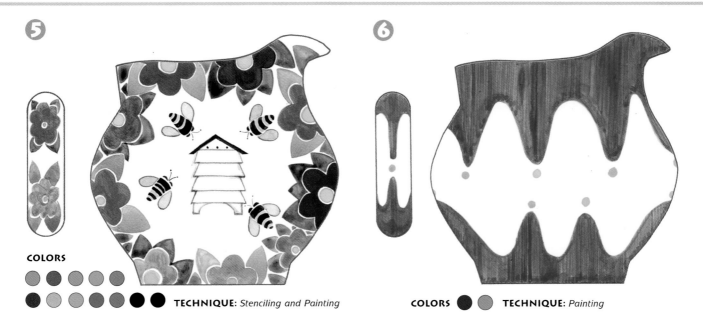

COLORS

● ● ● ● ●
● ● ● ● ● ● ● **TECHNIQUE:** *Stenciling and Painting*

6

COLORS ● ● **TECHNIQUE:** *Painting*

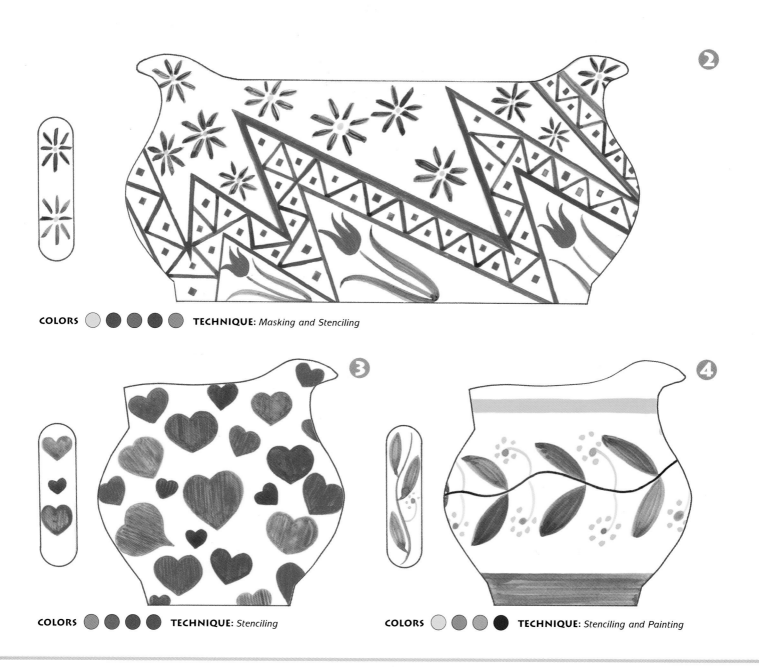

COLORS ○ ● ● ● ● **TECHNIQUE:** *Masking and Stenciling*

COLORS ● ● ● ● **TECHNIQUE:** *Stenciling*

COLORS ○ ● ● ● **TECHNIQUE:** *Stenciling and Painting*

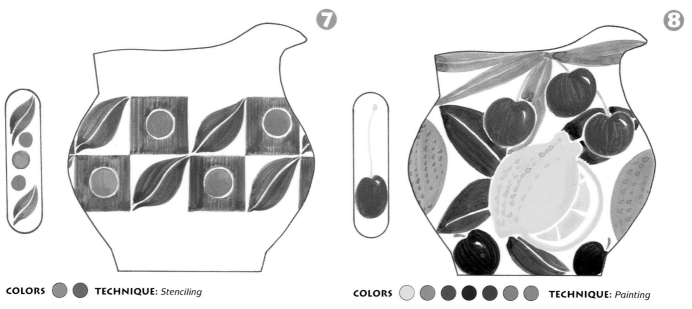

COLORS ● ● **TECHNIQUE:** *Stenciling*

COLORS ○ ● ● ● ● ● ● **TECHNIQUE:** *Painting*

51

LARGE **JUG**

BECAUSE OF ITS size and the visibility of its sides, the larger pitcher presents a great opportunity for creativity. These pages feature some very bold designs for you to copy. Designs 1 and 5 make wonderful use of color and can be very freely painted. Design 2 is perhaps the most complicated, and it may be best if you do it in three stages: first paint the middle band freehand, then stencil the flowers in the top band, and finally paint the lower band of fish. The melon slices of Design 6 can be created by stenciling and then painting the pips on top. The Christmas pudding and its vivid red background in Design 4, the blue diagonal abstract lines in Design 7, and the large flower in Design 8 can all be painted freely.

1

COLORS ●●●●●● **TECHNIQUE:** *Painting*

5

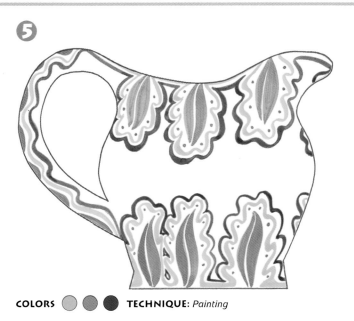

COLORS ●●● **TECHNIQUE:** *Painting*

6

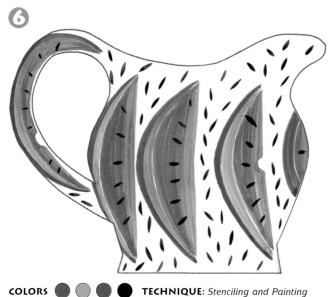

COLORS ●●●● **TECHNIQUE:** *Stenciling and Painting*

52

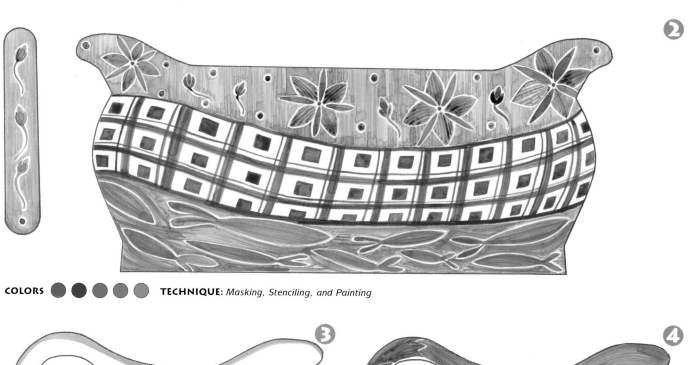

❷

COLORS ●●●●● **TECHNIQUE:** *Masking, Stenciling, and Painting*

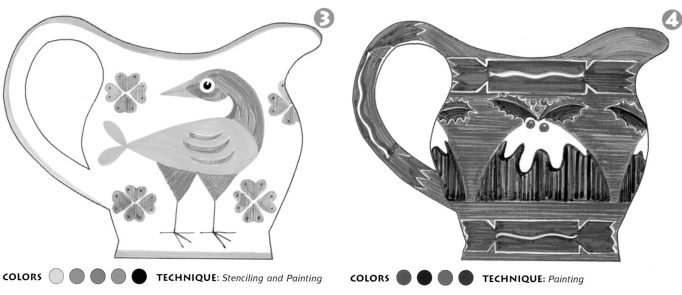

❸

COLORS ●●●●● **TECHNIQUE:** *Stenciling and Painting*

❹

COLORS ●●●● **TECHNIQUE:** *Painting*

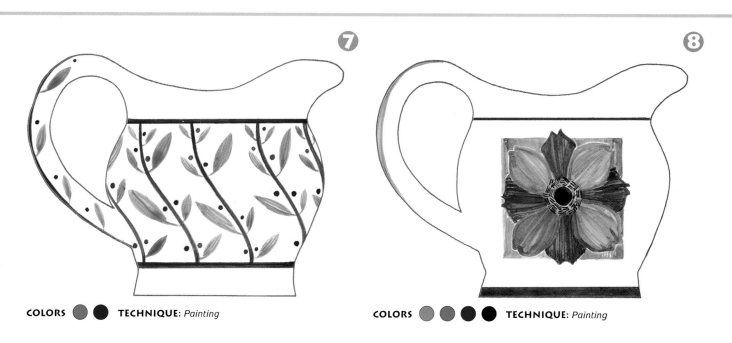

❼

COLORS ●● **TECHNIQUE:** *Painting*

❽

COLORS ●●●● **TECHNIQUE:** *Painting*

STRAIGHT-SIDED **JUG**

WHATEVER YOU USE *this pitcher for—an ornament, a flower vase, a container—there's no end to the variety of designs that flatter its shape. The magnificent thistles in Design 2 are best reproduced by combining the techniques of stenciling, sponging, and painting. The long-legged seagulls of Design 3 and the abstract decoration of Design 5 can be interpreted and painted freely, while the daffodils of Design 6 and the asparagus of Design 8 need to be painted more carefully. The diagonal geometric look of Design 4 requires accurate marking out if it is to retain its crispness.*

❶

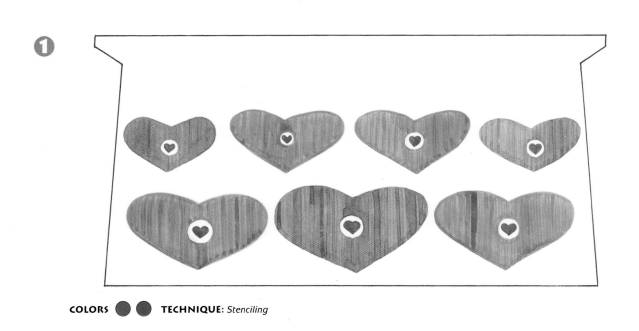

COLORS ● ● **TECHNIQUE:** *Stenciling*

❺

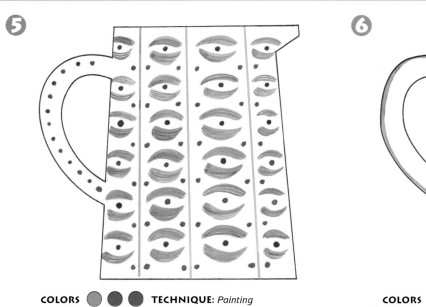

COLORS ● ● ● **TECHNIQUE:** *Painting*

❻

COLORS ● ● ● **TECHNIQUE:** *Painting*

54

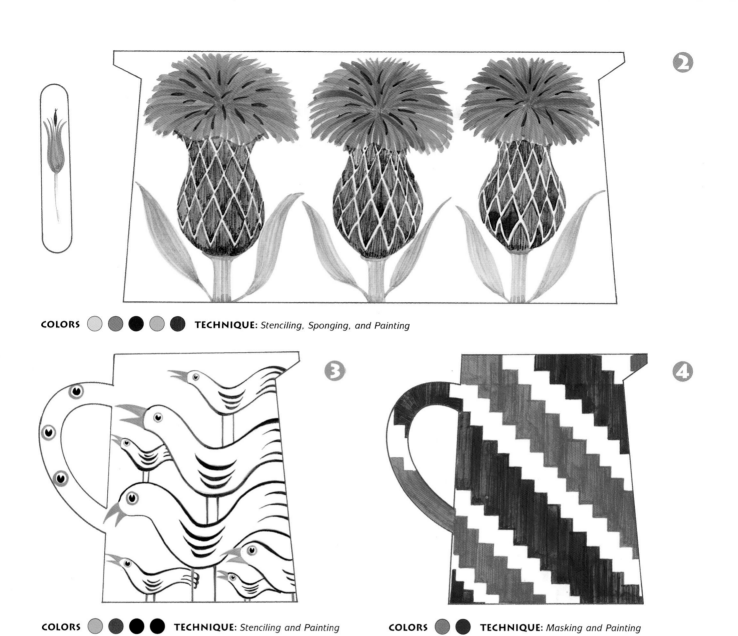

COLORS ● ● ● ● ●   **TECHNIQUE:** *Stenciling, Sponging, and Painting*

COLORS ● ● ● ●   **TECHNIQUE:** *Stenciling and Painting*

COLORS ● ●   **TECHNIQUE:** *Masking and Painting*

COLORS ● ●   **TECHNIQUE:** *Stenciling and Painting*

COLORS ● ● ● ●   **TECHNIQUE:** *Painting*

55

ROUND **TEAPOT 1**

THE FAMILIAR ROUND *teapot is so popular that we have four pages of designs to inspire you; its chubby, cheerful form cries out for lively decoration. The delightfully stylized butterflies of Design 1 are easy to reproduce with a combination of stenciling and painting. Design 7 is a personalized teapot for any Libran of your acquaintance—notice the smiling face in the design. Design 5 definitely looks more like an elephant than a teapot; the illusion is helped by carefully controling the direction of the brush strokes. When it comes to choosing a design for your teapot, keep in mind that you could use elements of it for the tea cups.*

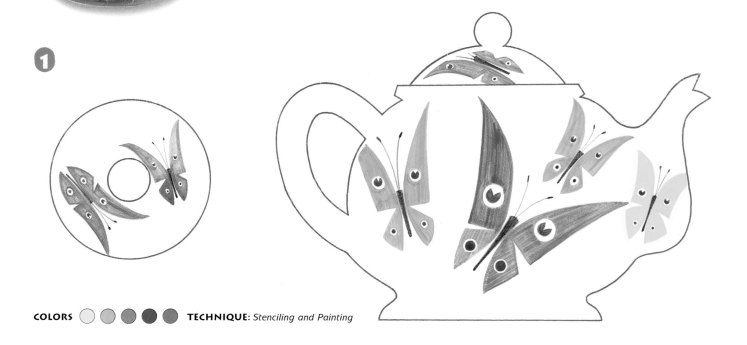

1

COLORS ●●●●● **TECHNIQUE:** *Stenciling and Painting*

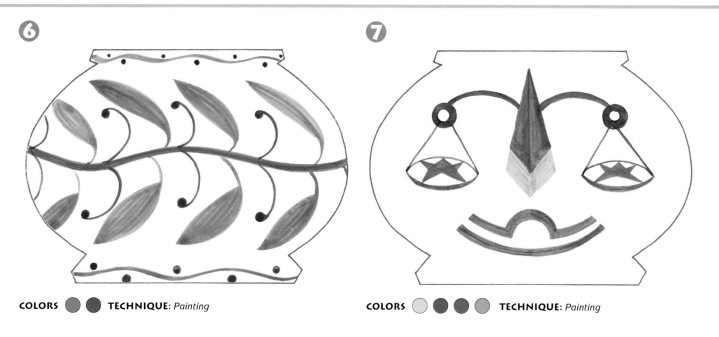

6

COLORS ●● **TECHNIQUE:** *Painting*

7

COLORS ●●●● **TECHNIQUE:** *Painting*

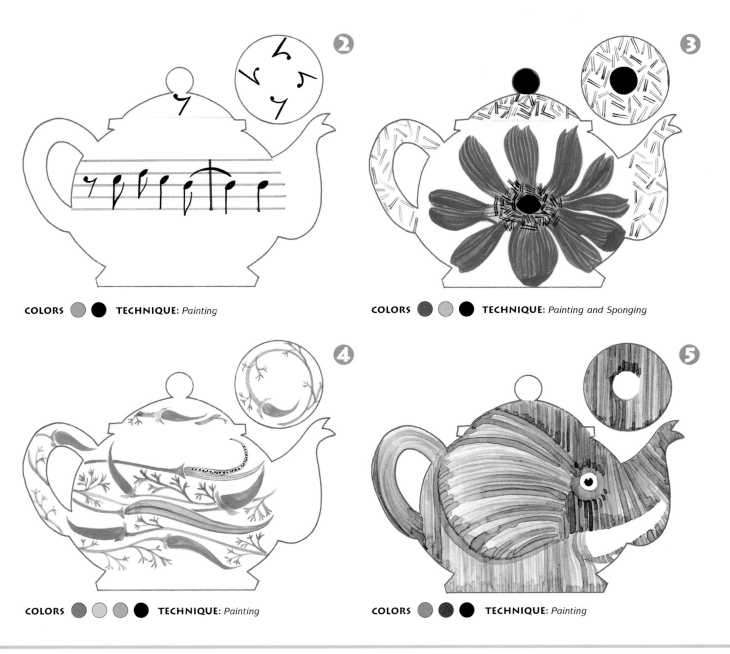

2

COLORS ⬤⬤ **TECHNIQUE:** *Painting*

3

COLORS ⬤⬤⬤ **TECHNIQUE:** *Painting and Sponging*

4

COLORS ⬤⬤⬤⬤ **TECHNIQUE:** *Painting*

5

COLORS ⬤⬤⬤ **TECHNIQUE:** *Painting*

8

COLORS ⬤⬤⬤⬤⬤⬤⬤⬤ **TECHNIQUE:** *Stenciling*

9

COLORS ⬤⬤⬤ **TECHNIQUE:** *Painting*

ROUND **TEAPOT 2**

MORE DESIGNS FOR *that family friend, the teapot! The runes (ancient lettering) used in Design 1 are also in the New Age theme section at the back of this book. The background of the runes can be stenciled, and the individual runes painted on afterward. When painting the tartan pattern in Design 2 remember to keep your brush strokes moving in the same direction. Once you have marked out your squares for Design 5, you can then paint in the lines. The simple abstract decoration of Design 6 combines stenciling and painting. Design 8 can be reproduced by stenciling, but let each color dry before applying the next.*

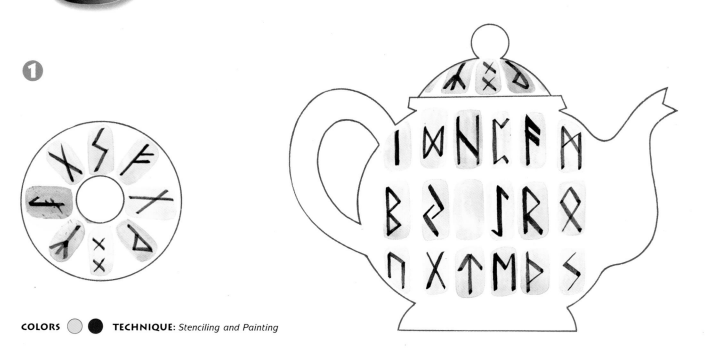

❶

COLORS ⚪ ⚫ **TECHNIQUE:** *Stenciling and Painting*

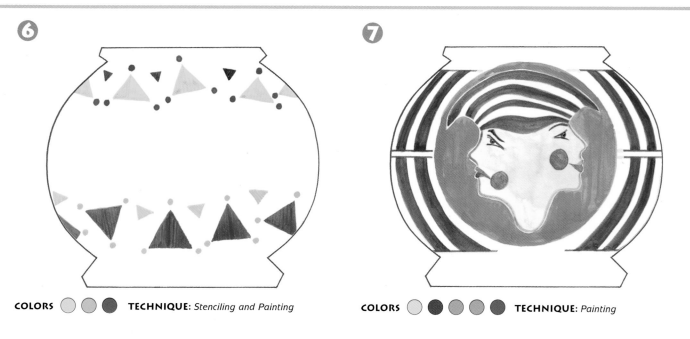

❻

COLORS ⚪ ⚪ ⚫ **TECHNIQUE:** *Stenciling and Painting*

❼

COLORS ⚪ ⚫ ⚫ ⚫ ⚫ **TECHNIQUE:** *Painting*

COLORS ⬤ ⬤ ⬤ **TECHNIQUE:** *Painting*

COLORS ○ ○ ⬤ ⬤ **TECHNIQUE:** *Stenciling and Painting*

COLORS ○ ⬤ ⬤ ⬤ ⬤ ⬤ ⬤ **TECHNIQUE:** *Painting*

COLORS ⬤ ⬤ **TECHNIQUE:** *Masking and Painting*

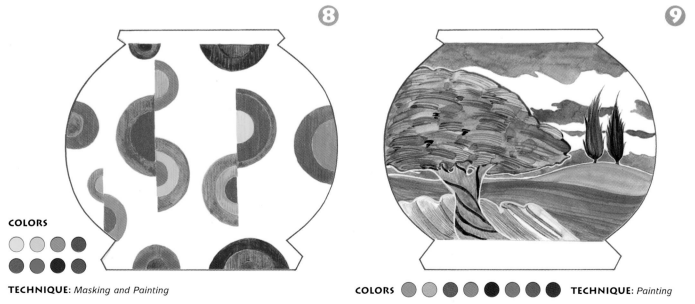

COLORS
○ ○ ⬤ ⬤
⬤ ⬤ ⬤ ⬤

TECHNIQUE: *Masking and Painting*

COLORS ⬤ ○ ⬤ ⬤ ⬤ ⬤ ⬤ ⬤ **TECHNIQUE:** *Painting*

STRAIGHT-SIDED **TEAPOT**

TAKE ADVANTAGE OF *the long, flat sides of this teapot when choosing your design, keeping in mind ideas for the handle and lid. All of these designs can be reproduced using painting or stenciling techniques. The design you choose will also be appropriate for straight-sided mugs should you want to have a matching set. On special occasions it's fun to have a special teapot with matching mugs, and Design 3 is perfect for the holiday season. The zebra pattern of Design 4 is definitely one for painting with care.*

❶

COLORS ● ● ● ● **TECHNIQUE:** *Painting*

❻

COLORS ○ ○ ● ● ● ● ● **TECHNIQUE:** *Stenciling*

❼

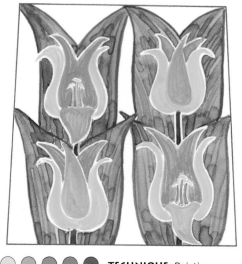

COLORS ○ ○ ● ● ● **TECHNIQUE:** *Painting*

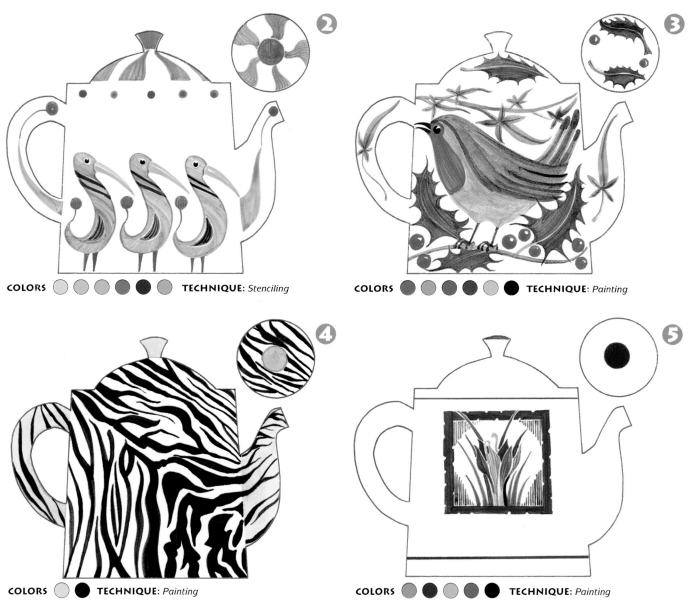

2

COLORS ● ● ● ● ● ● **TECHNIQUE:** *Stenciling*

3

COLORS ● ● ● ● ● ● **TECHNIQUE:** *Painting*

4

COLORS ● ● **TECHNIQUE:** *Painting*

5

COLORS ● ● ● ● ● **TECHNIQUE:** *Painting*

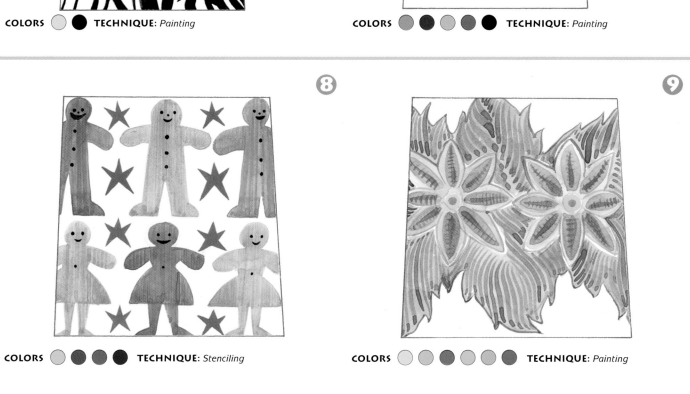

8

COLORS ● ● ● ● **TECHNIQUE:** *Stenciling*

9

COLORS ● ● ● ● ● ● **TECHNIQUE:** *Painting*

STRAIGHT-SIDED **COFFEE POT**

ALTHOUGH COFFEEPOTS DO *not tend to be as popular as teapots, it is still nice to have one for when you are entertaining friends and guests, which is all the more reason to make your design a talking point. There is a good selection of designs to choose from here, and most of them can be painted, although the playing card motifs of Design 2 and the ribbons and bows of Design 5 would reproduce well from stencils. The two tigers and the exotic jungle of Design 8 and the "Three Kings of the Orient" in Design 9 are for the more experienced painter.*

1

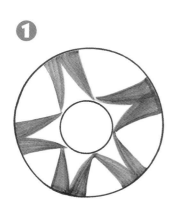

COLORS

TECHNIQUE: *Painting*

6

COLORS

TECHNIQUE:
Masking and Stenciling

7

COLORS

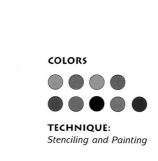

TECHNIQUE:
Stenciling and Painting

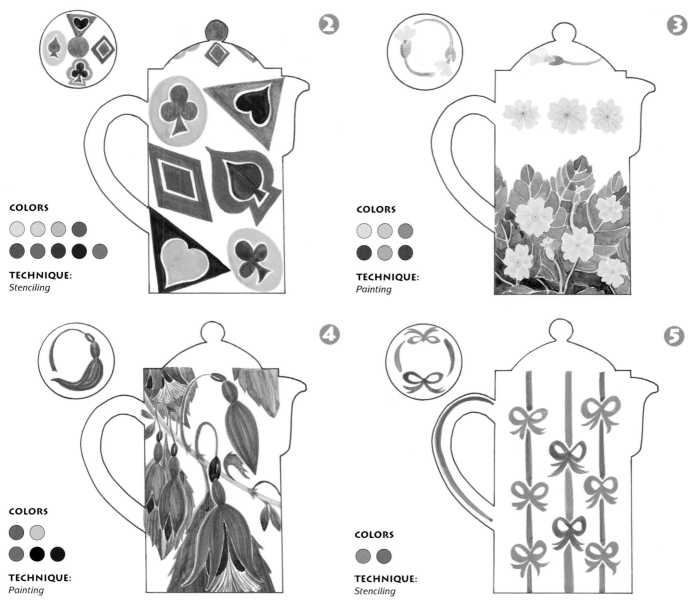

2

COLORS

TECHNIQUE:
Stenciling

3

COLORS

TECHNIQUE:
Painting

4

COLORS

TECHNIQUE:
Painting

5

COLORS

TECHNIQUE:
Stenciling

8

COLORS

TECHNIQUE:
Painting

9

COLORS

TECHNIQUE:
Painting

SAUCE/GRAVY BOAT & SAUCER

ALTHOUGH THE SAUCE *boat is a more traditional shape from fine china sets, it is a very useful item of tableware, especially when you are serving a roast dinner. A unique and colorful design will make this piece stand out on your table. Most of the patterns on these pages can be reproduced using painting or stenciling techniques. The two pigs in Design 4 and the delightful toucan in Design 8 could be stenciled first and then painted over with the details. The Persian-influenced pattern of Design 9 can be best achieved by a combination of stenciling and masking techniques.*

1

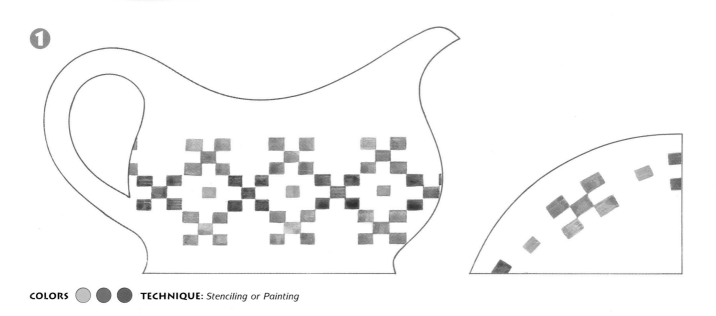

COLORS ⚪ ⚫ ⚫ **TECHNIQUE:** *Stenciling or Painting*

6

7

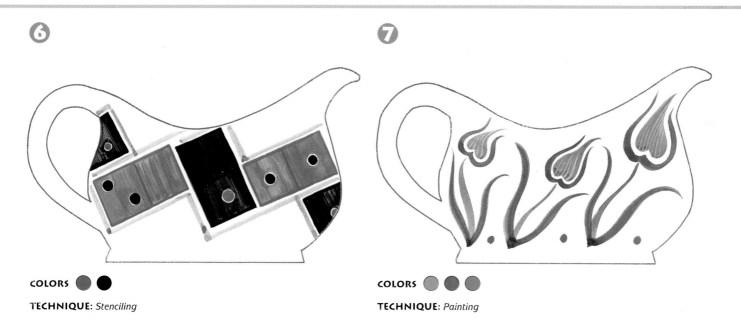

COLORS ⚫ ⚫

TECHNIQUE: *Stenciling*

COLORS ⚪ ⚫ ⚫

TECHNIQUE: *Painting*

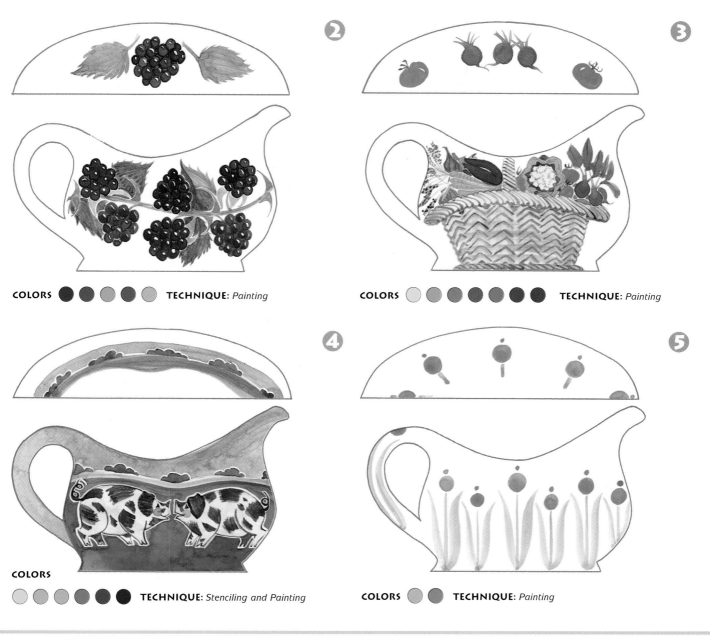

2

COLORS ● ● ● ● ○ **TECHNIQUE:** *Painting*

3

COLORS ○ ● ● ● ● ● ● **TECHNIQUE:** *Painting*

4

COLORS

○ ○ ● ● ● ● **TECHNIQUE:** *Stenciling and Painting*

5

COLORS ● ● **TECHNIQUE:** *Painting*

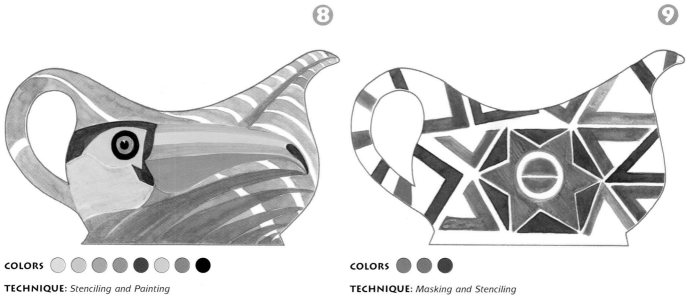

8

COLORS ○ ○ ○ ● ● ○ ● ●

TECHNIQUE: *Stenciling and Painting*

9

COLORS ● ● ●

TECHNIQUE: *Masking and Stenciling*

SMALL, CURVED **VASE**

THE ADVANTAGE OF *a vase shape is that there is no handle or spout, so the design isn't interrupted at any point. Many of us will have childhood memories of holidays spent at the seaside, and Design 1 attempts to recapture some of them. To apply the bright flowers of Design 2, use a combination of stenciling and sponging techniques. See how brightly colored the tropical fish is in Design 5; it looks as though it's swimming in the vase. The diagonally pointing triangles of Design 6 reproduce well using the stenciling technique.*

1

COLORS

TECHNIQUE:
Stenciling and Painting

5

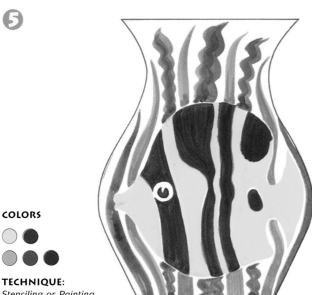

COLORS

TECHNIQUE:
Stenciling or Painting

6

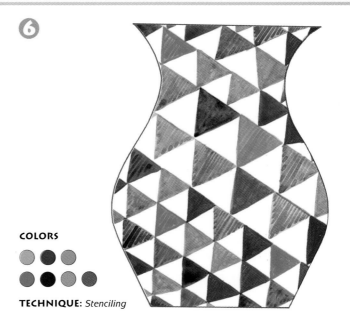

COLORS

TECHNIQUE: *Stenciling*

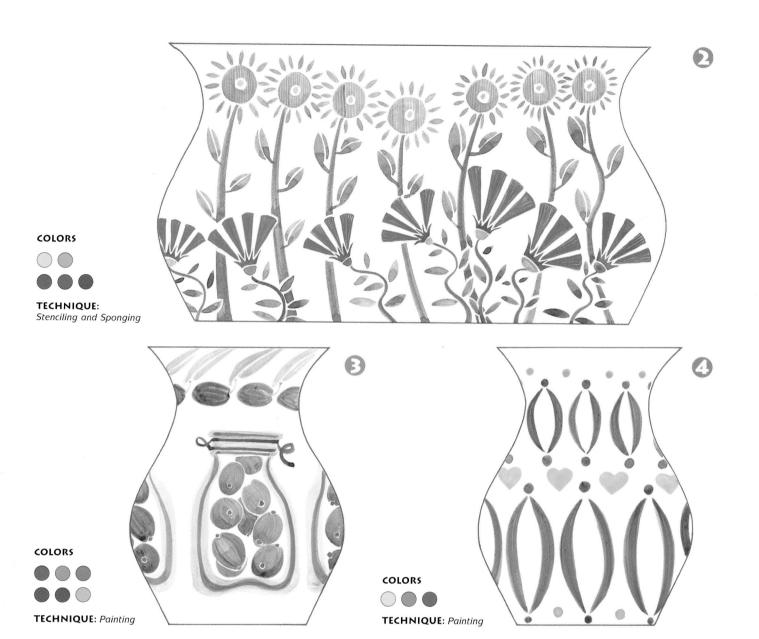

COLORS

TECHNIQUE:
Stenciling and Sponging

COLORS

TECHNIQUE: *Painting*

COLORS

TECHNIQUE: *Painting*

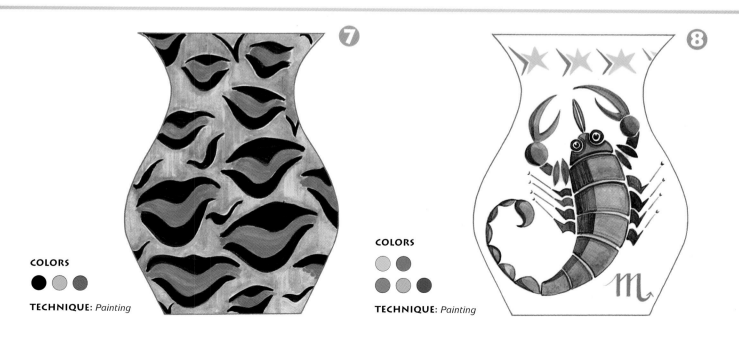

COLORS

TECHNIQUE: *Painting*

COLORS

TECHNIQUE: *Painting*

LARGE, CURVED VASE

THE GENEROUSLY SWOLLEN *sides of this vase are perfect for designs painted with thick, lush brush strokes. The inspiration for Design 1 comes from an ancient Celtic manuscript, while Design 5 has strong Venetian influences; both suit a combination of stenciling and painting techniques. Design 2, "Aquarius the Water Carrier," is a slightly more complicated design and should be painted with a certain amount of verve. You will need confident brushwork for the abstract pattern of Design 3, while the lemons of Design 8 will need stenciling before being painted over with the detail.*

①

COLORS

TECHNIQUE:
Stenciling and Painting

⑤

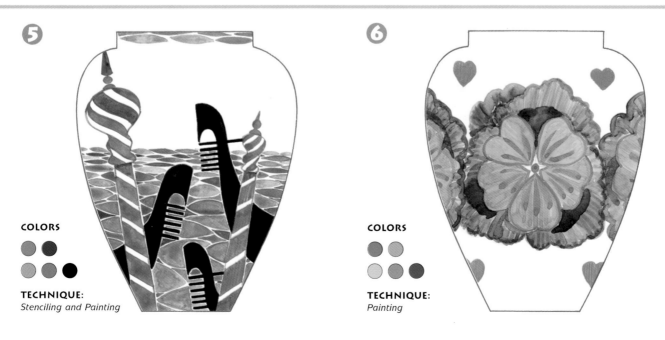

COLORS

TECHNIQUE:
Stenciling and Painting

⑥

COLORS

TECHNIQUE:
Painting

68

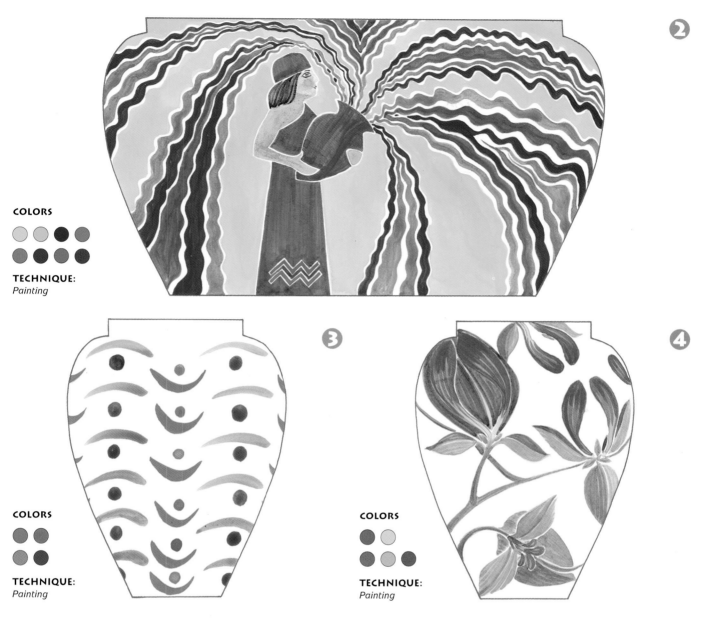

2

COLORS

TECHNIQUE:
Painting

3

COLORS

TECHNIQUE:
Painting

4

COLORS

TECHNIQUE:
Painting

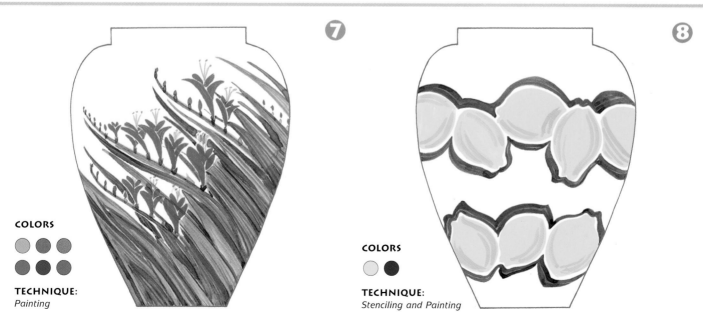

7

COLORS

TECHNIQUE:
Painting

8

COLORS

TECHNIQUE:
Stenciling and Painting

69

CONE **VASE**

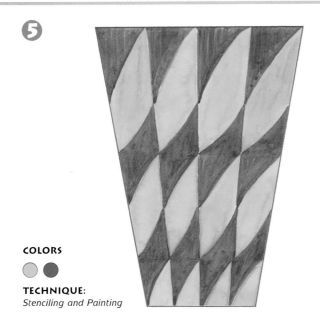

AS WITH THE cone-shaped mug and the beaker, the upside-down triangular shape of this vase lends itself to variations on the triangle theme. Painting is best for the intricate artwork of Design 2, which features a view through a window complete with drapes, and also for the pyramid of pears on a stand in Design 6. As always, remember to watch the direction of your brush strokes, as this makes all the difference to the final effect. The Taurean head of Design 4 and the diagonal abstract flowers of Design 7 can be achieved by stenciling and painting.

1

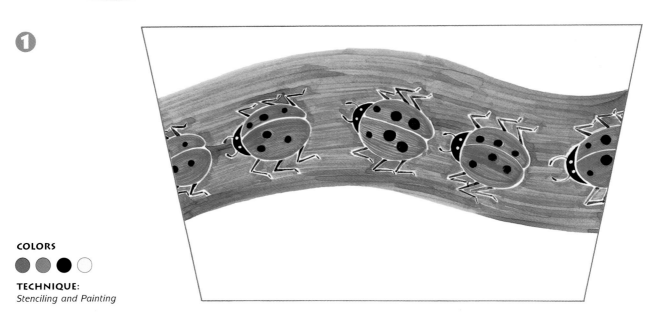

COLORS

TECHNIQUE:
Stenciling and Painting

5

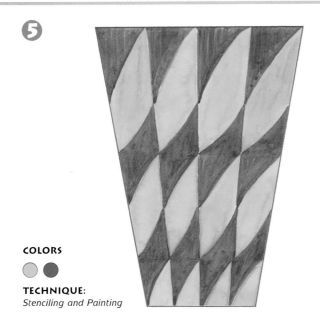

COLORS

TECHNIQUE:
Stenciling and Painting

6

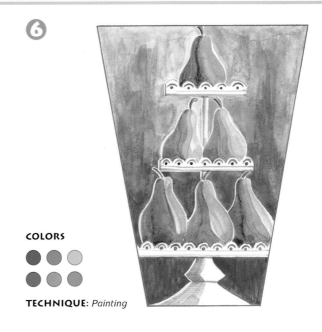

COLORS

TECHNIQUE: *Painting*

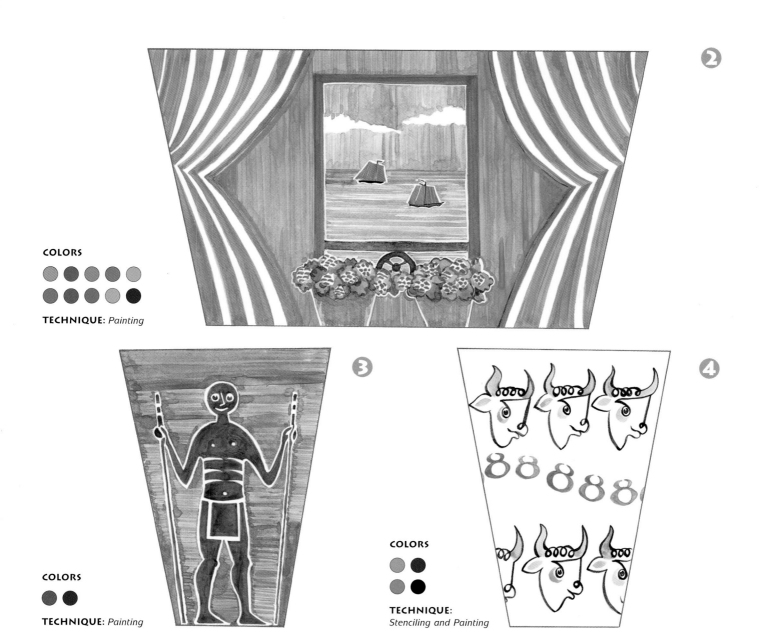

2

COLORS

TECHNIQUE: *Painting*

3

COLORS

TECHNIQUE: *Painting*

4

COLORS

TECHNIQUE:
Stenciling and Painting

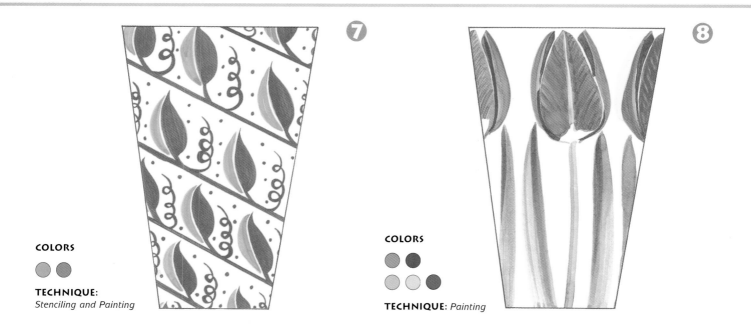

7

COLORS

TECHNIQUE:
Stenciling and Painting

8

COLORS

TECHNIQUE: *Painting*

OTHER TALL, SHAPED **VASES**

JUST AS THERE *is no end to the variety of vase shapes, so there is no end to the variety of designs you can create for them. Design 1 is for the gardeners among you and is suited to stenciling. The lilies of Design 2 were inspired by wall paintings from Knossos in Crete, and you can create them by stenciling and painting. As for Design 5, the more realistic the bamboo stalks are, the more striking the effect is; this design needs good painting skills. The abstract look of Design 6 can be best achieved by a combination of masking and painting.*

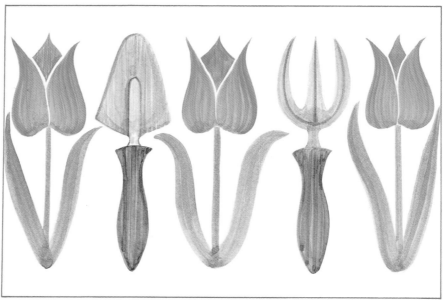

COLORS

TECHNIQUE: *Stenciling*

6

COLORS

TECHNIQUE:
Masking and Painting

7

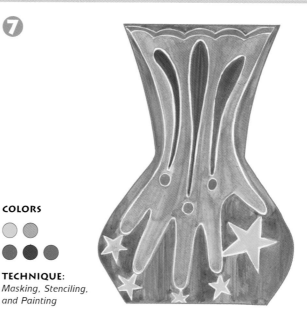

COLORS

TECHNIQUE:
*Masking, Stenciling,
and Painting*

②

COLORS

TECHNIQUE:
Stenciling and Painting

③

COLORS

TECHNIQUE:
Stenciling and Painting

④

COLORS

TECHNIQUE:
Stenciling and Painting

⑤

COLORS

TECHNIQUE:
Painting

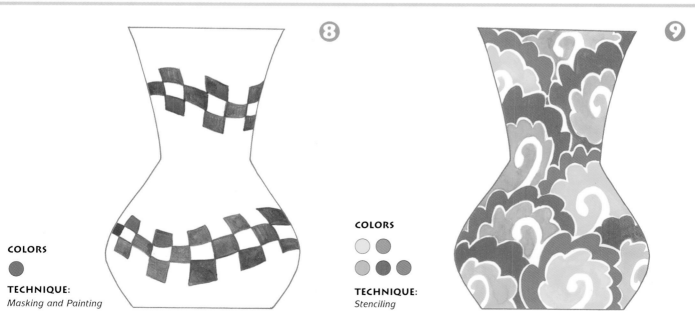

⑧

COLORS

TECHNIQUE:
Masking and Painting

⑨

COLORS

TECHNIQUE:
Stenciling

73

PLANTER

THE DESIGNS FOR *this deep planter give you the option of choosing a decoration that has a plant theme or a modern design. The fleur-de-lis of Design 1 can be stenciled, sponged, or painted, as can the diagonals of Design 8. The big flower in Design 2 can be achieved by combining stenciling and sponging, then painting over. Design 3 suits either stenciling or masking. The jester of Design 4 needs careful painting. The tulips of Design 5 and the parrots of Design 7 look good painted. Design 6 is easily stenciled. The angled checks of Design 9 are crisply achieved by careful masking.*

①

COLORS ● ● **TECHNIQUE:** *Stenciling or Sponging or Stamping and Painting*

⑥

⑦

COLORS ● ● ● **TECHNIQUE:** *Painting and Masking or Stenciling*   **COLORS** ● ● ● ● ● **TECHNIQUE:** *Painting and Stenciling*

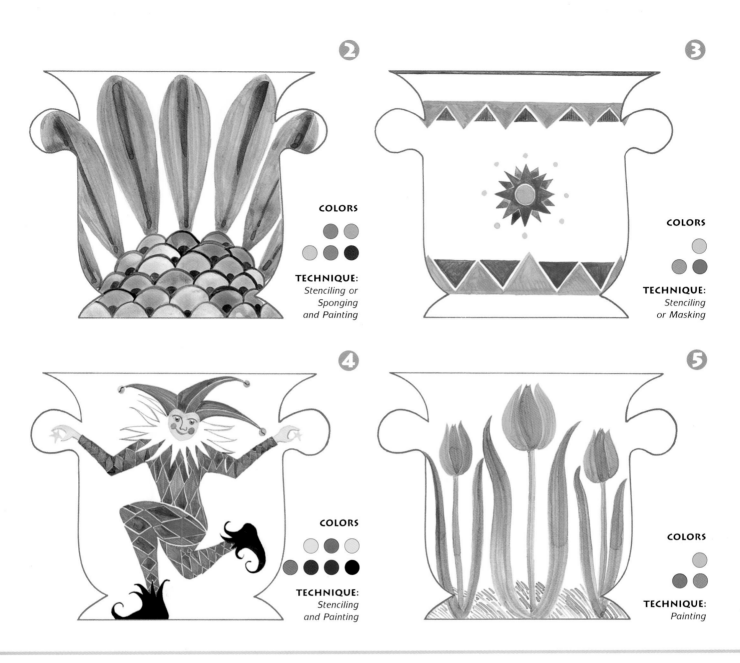

2

COLORS

TECHNIQUE:
*Stenciling or
Sponging
and Painting*

3

COLORS

TECHNIQUE:
*Stenciling
or Masking*

4

COLORS

TECHNIQUE:
*Stenciling
and Painting*

5

COLORS

TECHNIQUE:
Painting

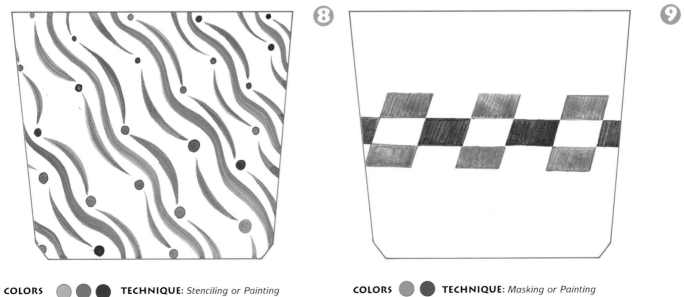

8

COLORS TECHNIQUE: *Stenciling or Painting*

9

COLORS TECHNIQUE: *Masking or Painting*

EGGCUP

EGG CUPS ARE *fun to decorate, as shown by Designs 1 and 2. Design 1 makes a cheery face to greet you as you eat your boiled egg in the morning, and is easily created by stenciling and painting, as are the chicks on Design 4. The broken-edged eggshell of Design 3 is achieved by masking and painting, while Humpty Dumpty in Design 2 and the geometric pattern of Design 9 look best painted. The bold checks and cross of Design 5 can be stenciled, as can the variation on the fleur-de-lis theme of Design 6 and the eyes of Design 8. Design 7 combines stenciling with masking.*

❶

COLORS ⬤⬤⬤ **TECHNIQUE:** *Stenciling and Painting*

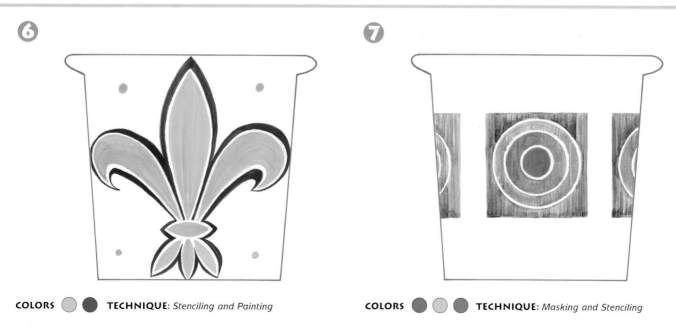

❻

COLORS ⬤⬤ **TECHNIQUE:** *Stenciling and Painting*

❼

COLORS ⬤⬤⬤ **TECHNIQUE:** *Masking and Stenciling*

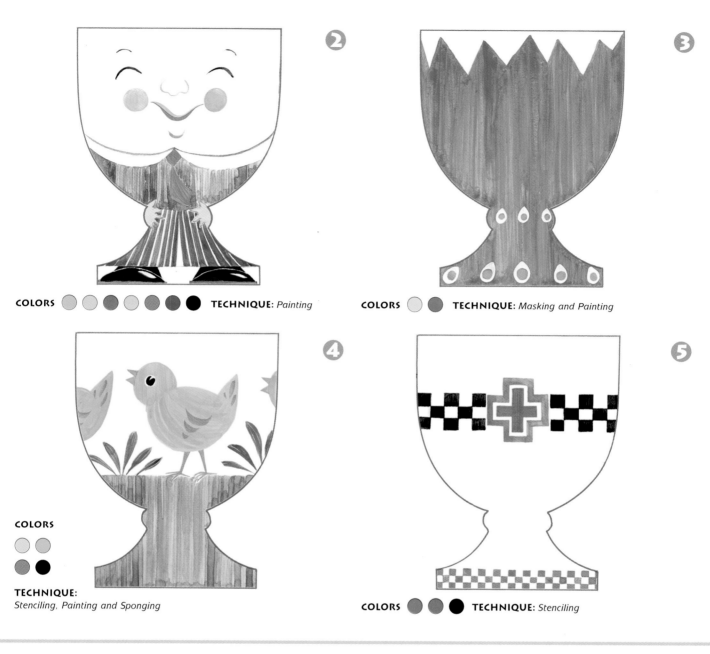

2

COLORS ⚪⚪🔵🔵🔵🔵⚫ **TECHNIQUE:** *Painting*

3

COLORS ⚪🔵 **TECHNIQUE:** *Masking and Painting*

4

COLORS
⚪⚪
🔵⚫

TECHNIQUE:
Stenciling, Painting and Sponging

5

COLORS 🔵🔵⚫ **TECHNIQUE:** *Stenciling*

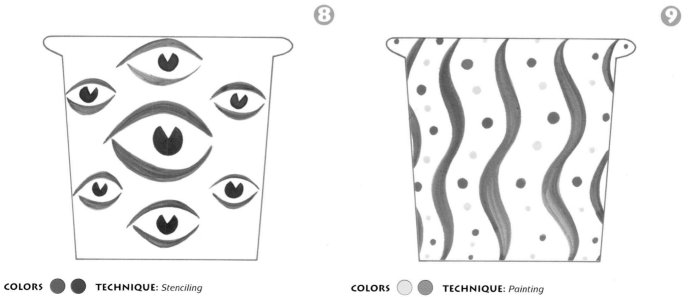

8

COLORS 🔵🔵 **TECHNIQUE:** *Stenciling*

9

COLORS ⚪🔵 **TECHNIQUE:** *Painting*

SALT AND PEPPER **CRUET SET**

ONE OF THE good things about designing items which are used as a pair is to keep them similar yet different in some way. Salt and pepper come in many different shapes and sizes, so there is scope for you to come up with your own innovative ideas. Here are some simple, easy designs to start you off. Designs 1, 3, 8, and 9 are all easily achieved by using a stencil. The owls of Design 2 and the sunflowers of Design 7 are best created by painting. The ivy leaves of Design 4 could have their outlines stenciled and then filled in by painting. The patriotic Stars and Stripes of Design 5 and the crazy paving of Design 6 are best suited to first masking and then stenciling.

➊

COLORS ◯ ◯ ◯ ● ◯ **TECHNIQUE:** *Stenciling*

➏

➐

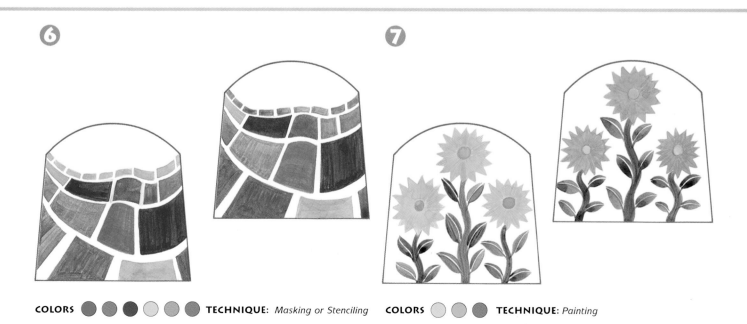

COLORS ● ● ● ◯ ◯ ◯ **TECHNIQUE:** *Masking or Stenciling*   **COLORS** ◯ ◯ ● **TECHNIQUE:** *Painting*

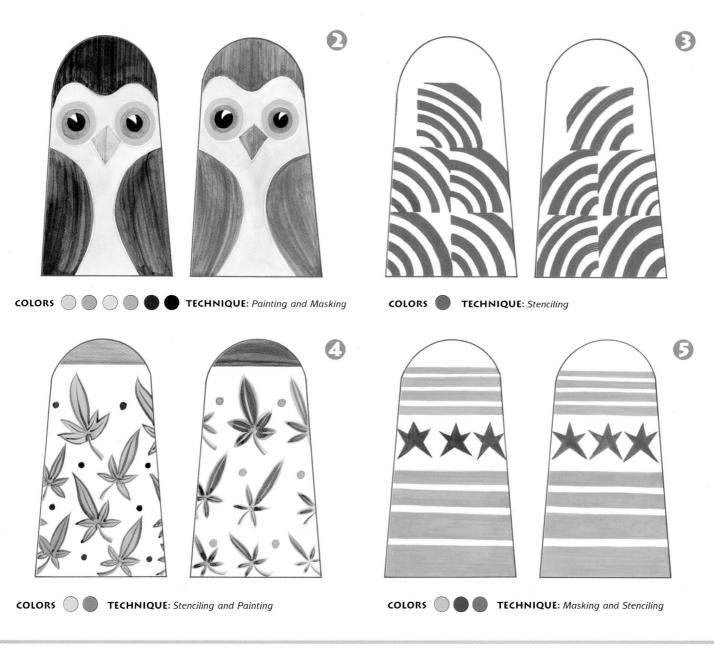

COLORS ⬤⬤⬤⬤⬤⬤ **TECHNIQUE:** *Painting and Masking*

COLORS ⬤ **TECHNIQUE:** *Stenciling*

COLORS ⬤⬤ **TECHNIQUE:** *Stenciling and Painting*

COLORS ⬤⬤⬤ **TECHNIQUE:** *Masking and Stenciling*

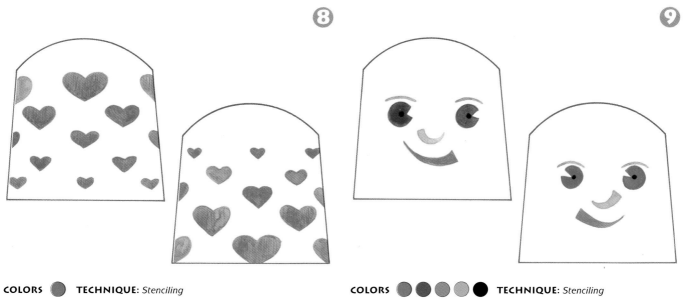

COLORS ⬤ **TECHNIQUE:** *Stenciling*

COLORS ⬤⬤⬤⬤⬤ **TECHNIQUE:** *Stenciling*

MUSTARD POT

THE HUMBLE MUSTARD *pot is often overlooked, which is all the more reason to make it stand out on the table with some really distinctive ideas. Notice how the lid can be incorporated into the design. As you will see, most of these designs can be created using a combination of painting and stenciling. The elephant of Design 7 can be painted, although for a softer effect you can use a stencil and sponge for the body color. The pink flowers of Design 8 can range freely over all the pot.*

①

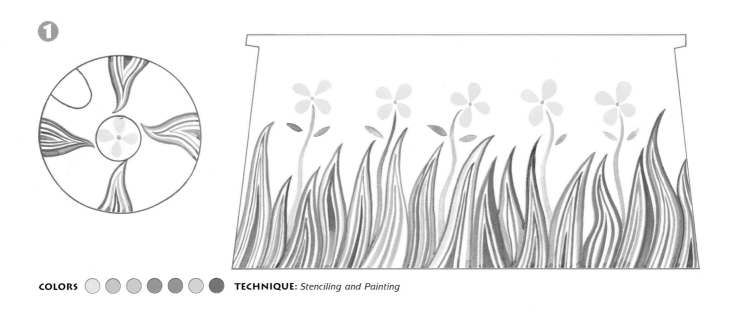

COLORS ○○○○○○○ **TECHNIQUE:** *Stenciling and Painting*

⑥ **⑦**

COLORS ○○ **TECHNIQUE:** *Stenciling and Painting*   **COLORS** ○○○○●● **TECHNIQUE:** *Painting or Sponging*

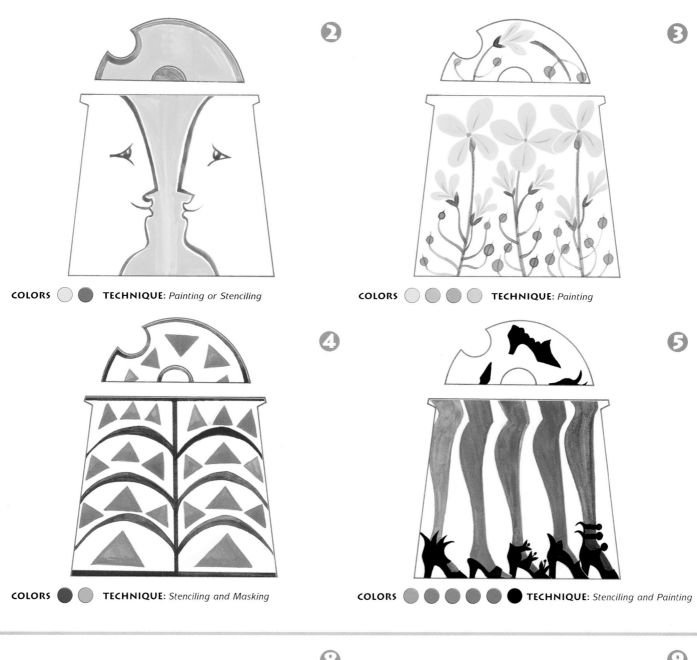

COLORS ○ ● TECHNIQUE: *Painting or Stenciling*

COLORS ○ ○ ○ ○ TECHNIQUE: *Painting*

COLORS ● ○ TECHNIQUE: *Stenciling and Masking*

COLORS ○ ○ ○ ○ ○ ● TECHNIQUE: *Stenciling and Painting*

COLORS ○ ● ● TECHNIQUE: *Painting*

COLORS ● ○ TECHNIQUE: *Stenciling and Painting*

81

SMALL, LIDDED **STORAGE/SPICE JAR**

IN THE CASE *of some shapes, you can have fun in coming up with a design that relates to its actual use. For example, for this spice jar we suggest some hot and "spicy" colors. You might even prefer to make them hotter still! The simple stenciled flowers of Design 7 might be easy to start with, followed by the abstract patterns of Designs 4 and 5. Designs 1, 2, and 6 are, again, fairly straightforward. The leopard in Design 8 isn't as complicated as you might think; just take it slowly and break the design down into its separate parts.*

❶

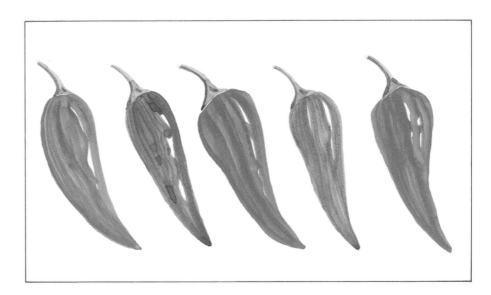

COLORS ⬤ ⬤   **TECHNIQUE:** *Painting*

❻

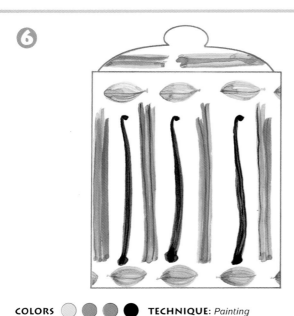

COLORS ⬤ ⬤ ⬤ ⬤   **TECHNIQUE:** *Painting*

❼

COLORS ⬤ ⬤   **TECHNIQUE:** *Stenciling*

2

COLORS

TECHNIQUE: *Painting and Sponging*

3

COLORS

TECHNIQUE:
Painting and Stenciling

4

COLORS **TECHNIQUE**: *Masking and Stenciling*

5

COLORS **TECHNIQUE**: *Painting and Stenciling*

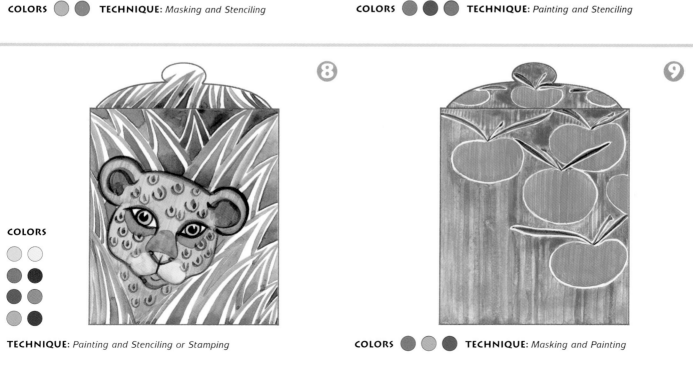

8

COLORS

TECHNIQUE: *Painting and Stenciling or Stamping*

9

COLORS **TECHNIQUE**: *Masking and Painting*

83

LARGE LIDDED **STORAGE JAR**

ONCE AGAIN, THIS *storage jar has a large area available for design and the temptation might be to use designs with a food theme, but try not to limit yourself. Remember, the design on the lid will add a nice touch that completes the effect. Design 1 should be the easiest to do. The peasant woman of Design 3 is not as intricate as she might appear at first glance, and the smiling ice-cream wafers of Design 4 look as good on the lid of the pot as they do on the sides. There are a variety of ways in which you could recreate the corncobs of Design 6. The pattern of the fritillaries on Design 8 is echoed in the pattern on the lid.*

1

COLORS ⚪⚪⚫⚫⚫ **TECHNIQUE:** *Stenciling and Painting*

6

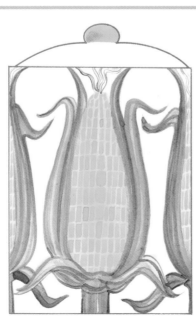

COLORS
⚪⚪⚫
⚪⚫⚫

TECHNIQUE:
*Painting and
Stenciling or
Sponging or Stamping*

7

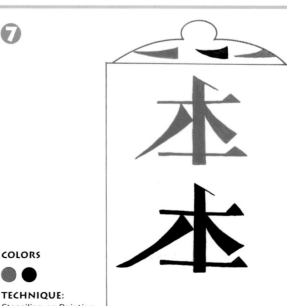

COLORS
⚫⚫

TECHNIQUE:
Stenciling or Painting

84

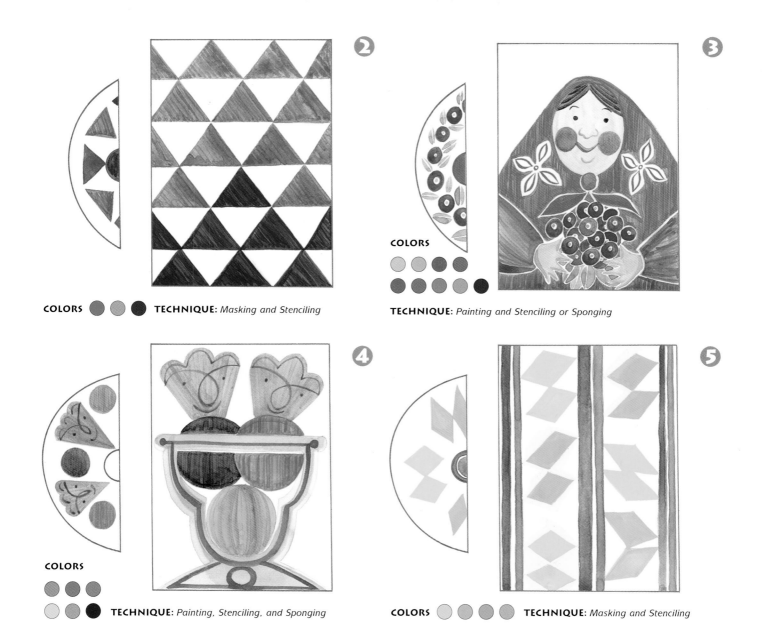

2

COLORS ● ● ● **TECHNIQUE:** *Masking and Stenciling*

3

COLORS
● ● ● ●
● ● ● ● ●

TECHNIQUE: *Painting and Stenciling or Sponging*

4

COLORS
● ● ●
● ● ●

TECHNIQUE: *Painting, Stenciling, and Sponging*

5

COLORS ● ● ● ● **TECHNIQUE:** *Masking and Stenciling*

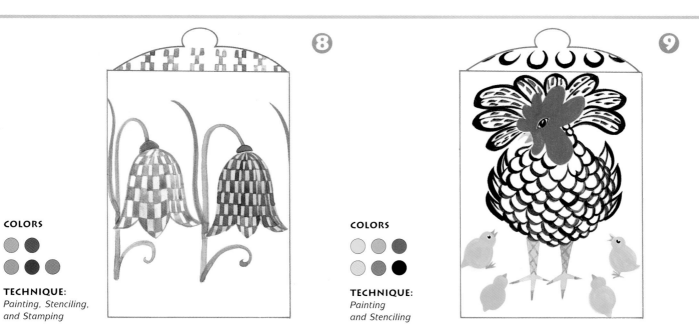

8

COLORS
● ●
● ● ●

TECHNIQUE:
*Painting, Stenciling,
and Stamping*

9

COLORS
● ● ●
● ● ●

TECHNIQUE:
*Painting
and Stenciling*

BUTTER **DISH**

SINCE THE BUTTER dish usually makes its appearance at the table in the morning, here are a couple of designs based on the theme of sunshine. The sunny colors of Design 1 and the sunrise of Design 7 should both be easy to execute, as should the more abstract lines of Design 8. Designs 2, 3, 4, and 6 all use a combination of stencil work and painting. You could incorporate sponging into the Egyptian lotus flowers and their leaves in Design 2. The bluey purples of the lavender flowers in Design 9 are reminiscent of summers in the South of France.

1

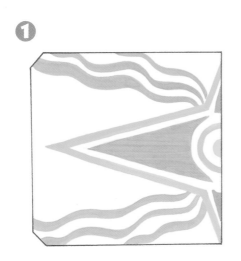

COLORS ○ ○ ● **TECHNIQUE:** *Stenciling and Painting*

6   **7**

COLORS ○ ○ ● ● ● **TECHNIQUE:** *Stenciling and Painting*   **COLORS** ○ ○ ● ● **TECHNIQUE:** *Masking and Stenciling*

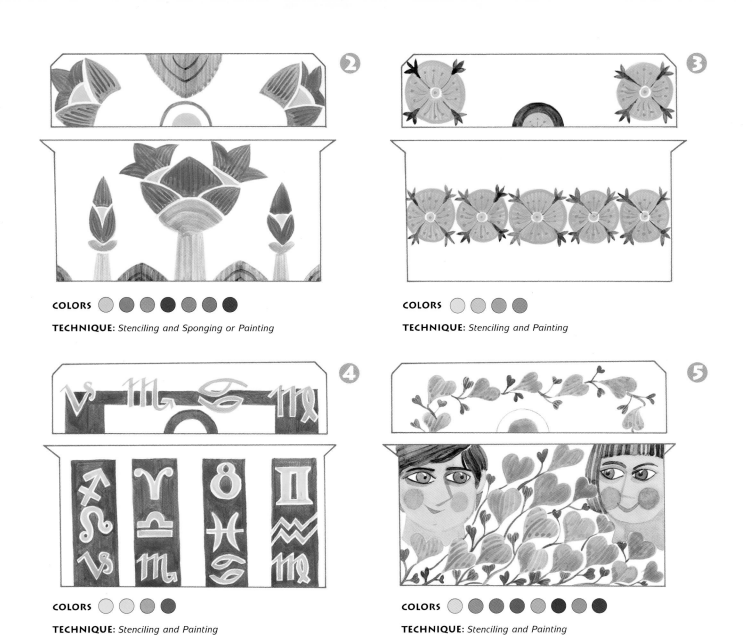

COLORS ○ ● ● ● ● ● ●

TECHNIQUE: *Stenciling and Sponging or Painting*

COLORS ○ ○ ○ ●

TECHNIQUE: *Stenciling and Painting*

COLORS ○ ○ ○ ●

TECHNIQUE: *Stenciling and Painting*

COLORS ○ ● ● ● ● ● ● ● ●

TECHNIQUE: *Stenciling and Painting*

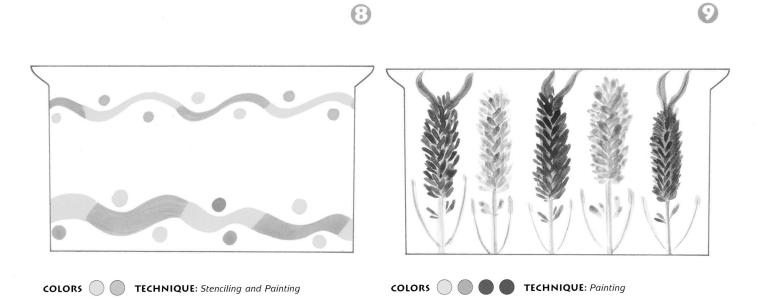

COLORS ○ ● **TECHNIQUE:** *Stenciling and Painting*

COLORS ○ ● ● ● **TECHNIQUE:** *Painting*

CHEESE **DISH**

A CHEESE DISH offers a nice, chunky area to decorate, and the opportunity to work on several surfaces. In Design 1, what better accompaniment for your selection of cheeses than grapes? Design 2 is similar to one of the designs for the egg cups, which shows how some designs transfer easily to different objects. Designs 3, 4, and 5 are possibly the easiest to try. You could even pretend that the dish itself is made of cheese, as in Design 6. We all know that mice love cheese, so here they are in Design 7. Designs 8 and 9 will work well with stenciling and painting.

1

COLORS ●●●●○●●● **TECHNIQUE:** Painting, Stenciling, and Sponging

6

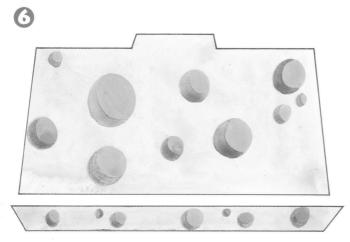

COLORS
○○○

TECHNIQUE: Stenciling and Painting

7

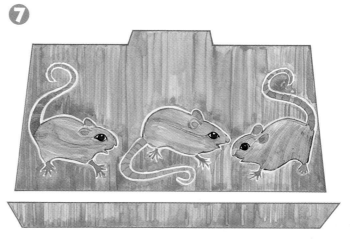

COLORS
○○○○●

TECHNIQUE: Painting and Sponging

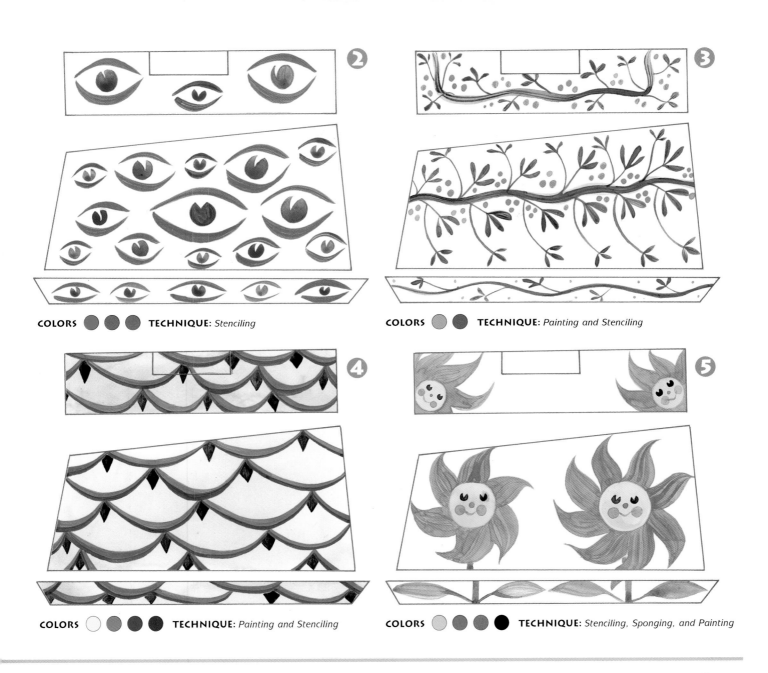

COLORS ● ● ● **TECHNIQUE:** *Stenciling*

COLORS ● ● **TECHNIQUE:** *Painting and Stenciling*

COLORS ○ ● ● ● **TECHNIQUE:** *Painting and Stenciling*

COLORS ○ ● ● ● **TECHNIQUE:** *Stenciling, Sponging, and Painting*

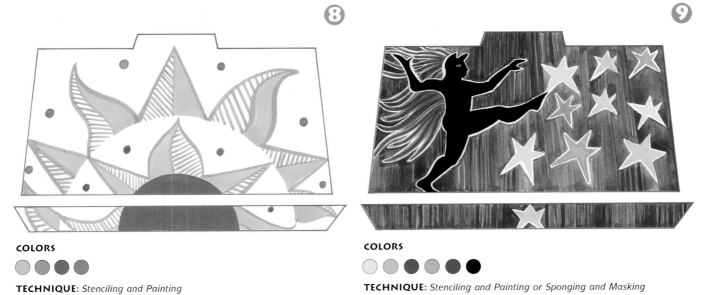

COLORS

● ● ● ●

TECHNIQUE: *Stenciling and Painting*

COLORS

○ ● ● ● ● ●

TECHNIQUE: *Stenciling and Painting or Sponging and Masking*

ROUND VEGETABLE **TUREEN**

ALTHOUGH THIS IS *a tureen for vegetables, it can also be used for pasta or stews and casseroles or even fruit and puddings. So your designs can reflect a multiple of themes. Designs 1, 2, 4, and 7 are the easier designs for the vegetable tureen. For the Capricorn goat in Design 3, mask out the central icon and stencil in the figures; then the goat can be painted or stenciled. The Italian landscape of Design 6 should be broken down into several stages. The fishes of Design 8 can be done by masking and painting, as can the vegetables of Design 9.*

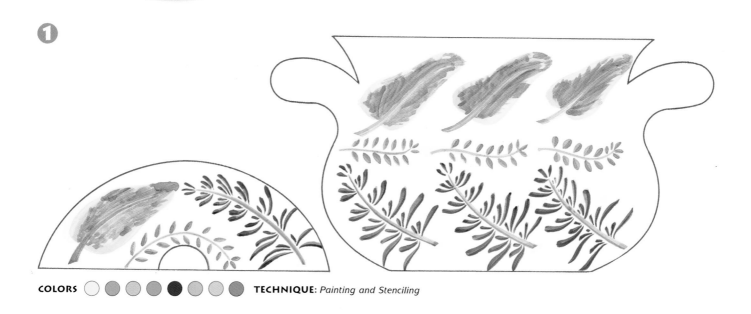

1

COLORS ○ ○ ○ ○ ○ ● ○ ○ ○   **TECHNIQUE:** *Painting and Stenciling*

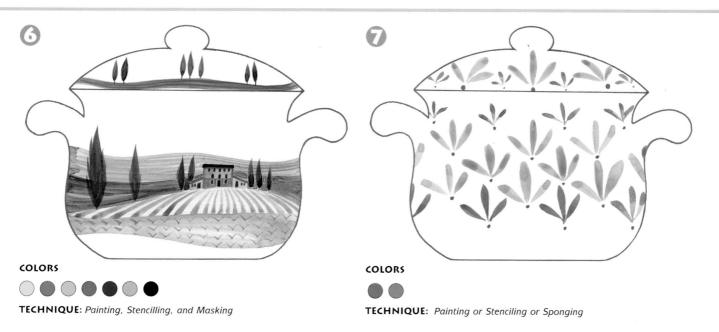

6

COLORS
○ ○ ○ ○ ● ○ ●

TECHNIQUE: *Painting, Stencilling, and Masking*

7

COLORS
● ●

TECHNIQUE: *Painting or Stenciling or Sponging*

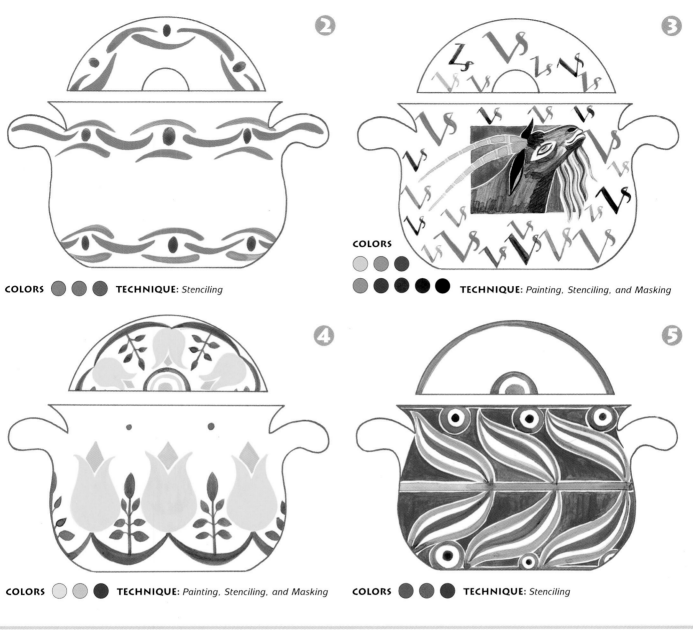

COLORS ⬤⬤⬤ **TECHNIQUE:** *Stenciling*

COLORS
◯⬤⬤
⬤⬤⬤⬤⬤ **TECHNIQUE:** *Painting, Stenciling, and Masking*

COLORS ◯◯⬤ **TECHNIQUE:** *Painting, Stenciling, and Masking*

COLORS ⬤⬤⬤ **TECHNIQUE:** *Stenciling*

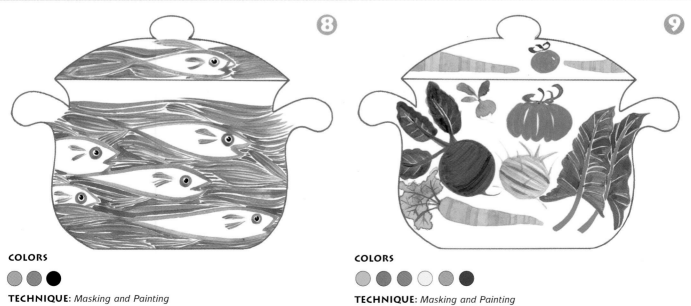

COLORS
⬤⬤⬤

TECHNIQUE: *Masking and Painting*

COLORS
⬤⬤⬤◯⬤⬤

TECHNIQUE: *Masking and Painting*

91

LARGE ROASTING **DISH**

THE VERY EASIEST decoration is Design 4 with its vertical stripes and dots, which can be created by masking and stenciling. The same techniques can also be used for the profiles of the men in Design 3, the wavy line of triangles in Design 7, and the Stars and Stripes of Design 9. Designs 1, 6, and 8 are slightly more complicated and are best suited to painting. The dove of peace surrounded by hearts, Design 2, can be created by stenciling and painting. If you try Design 5, use the sides of two differently sized brushes.

①

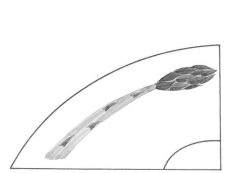

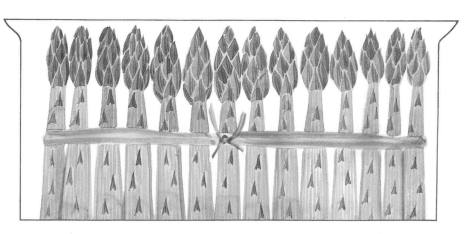

COLORS ⚪⚪⚫⚫ **TECHNIQUE:** *Painting*

---

⑥

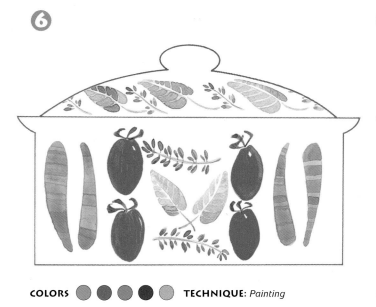

COLORS ⚫⚫⚫⚫⚪ **TECHNIQUE:** *Painting*

⑦

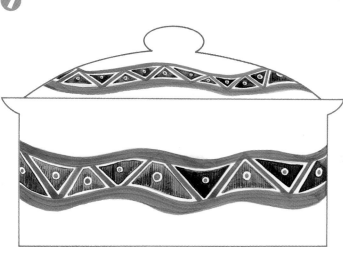

COLORS ⚫⚫⚫ **TECHNIQUE:** *Masking, Painting, and Stenciling*

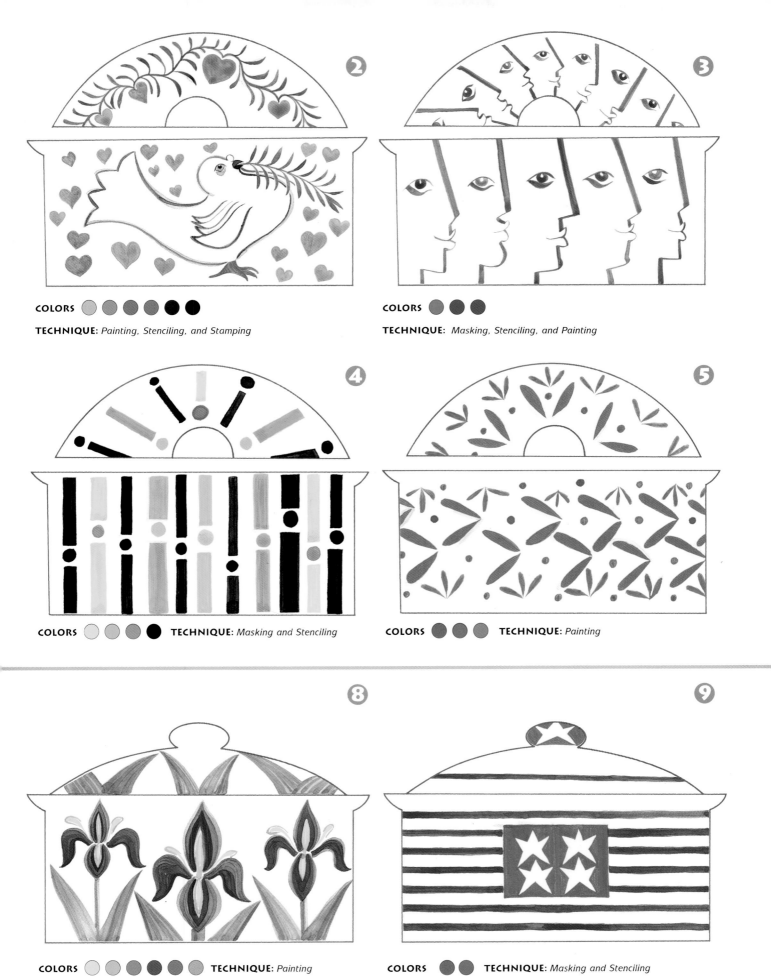

2

COLORS ● ● ● ● ● ●

TECHNIQUE: *Painting, Stenciling, and Stamping*

3

COLORS ● ● ●

TECHNIQUE: *Masking, Stenciling, and Painting*

4

COLORS ● ● ● ● **TECHNIQUE:** *Masking and Stenciling*

5

COLORS ● ● ● **TECHNIQUE:** *Painting*

8

COLORS ● ● ● ● ● ● **TECHNIQUE:** *Painting*

9

COLORS ● ● **TECHNIQUE:** *Masking and Stenciling*

SMALL, ROUND **PLATE**

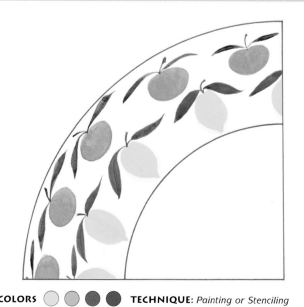

WITH MOST PLATES *it is generally best to keep the decoration to the rims, so that the designs aren't scratched by cutlery. Designs 1 and 5 have simple and effective flowers which can be created by stenciling in the usual way, or by sponging through a stencil, and they are easy enough to give the beginner confidence. Design 2 benefits from a carefully cut stencil, while a little more care is needed for the straight lines of Design 6. Designs 4, 5, and 8 can all be made with the use of stencils and very easy painting.*

1

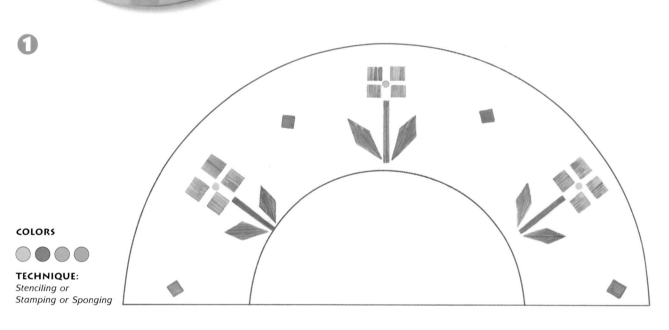

COLORS

TECHNIQUE:
Stenciling or Stamping or Sponging

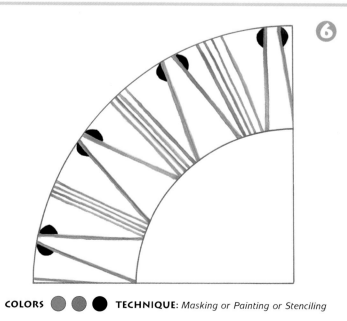

5

6

COLORS **TECHNIQUE:** *Painting or Stenciling*

COLORS **TECHNIQUE:** *Masking or Painting or Stenciling*

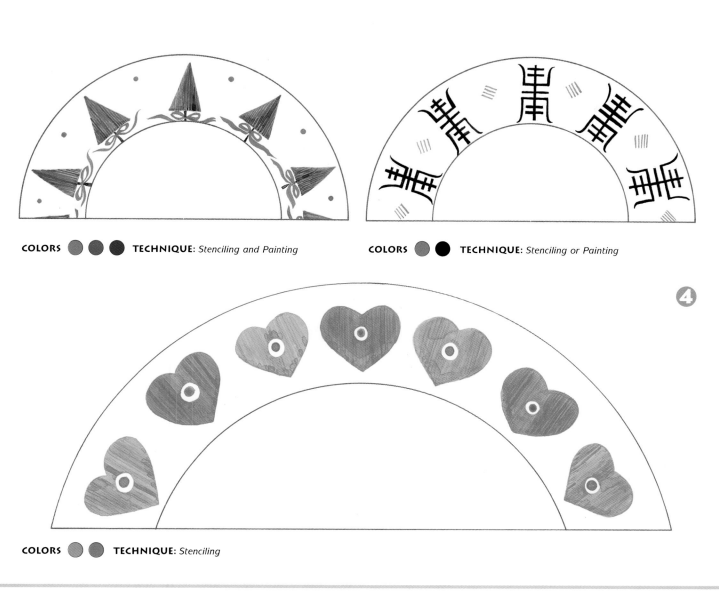

2

COLORS ● ● ● **TECHNIQUE:** *Stenciling and Painting*

3

COLORS ● ● **TECHNIQUE:** *Stenciling or Painting*

4

COLORS ● ● **TECHNIQUE:** *Stenciling*

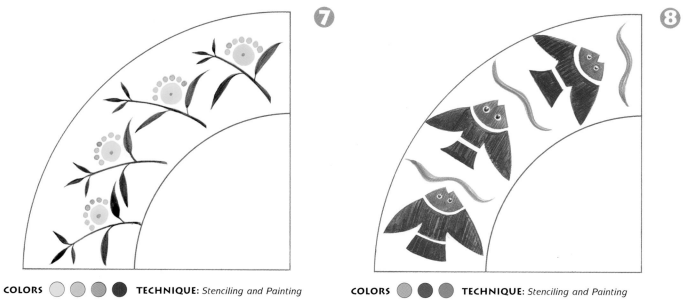

7

COLORS ● ● ● ● **TECHNIQUE:** *Stenciling and Painting*

8

COLORS ● ● ● **TECHNIQUE:** *Stenciling and Painting*

95

MEDIUM, ROUND **PLATE**

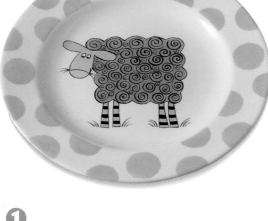

A FRESH AND *simple design to start with: lemon and lime segments, easily created by using a stencil with or without a sponge. Designs 2, 3, and 4 are all very bold and colorful and can be reproduced using a stencil in conjunction with either masking or painting. Designs 5 and 6 are both fairly straightforward and can be created with a stencil. The owls and branches of Design 7 can be achieved by using a stencil and then painting over, as can the smiling masks of Design 8.*

1

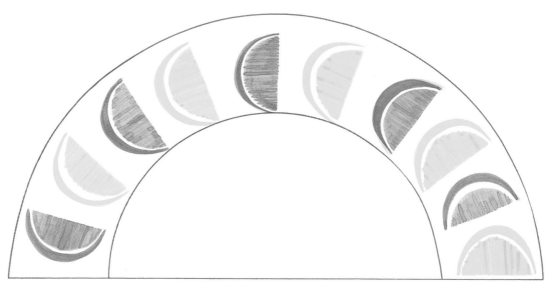

COLORS

TECHNIQUE:
*Stenciling or
Stamping or Sponging*

5

COLORS ● **TECHNIQUE:** *Stenciling or Masking and Painting*

6

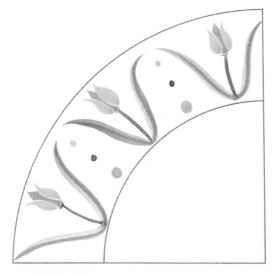

COLORS ○ ○ ○ **TECHNIQUE:** *Stenciling and Painting*

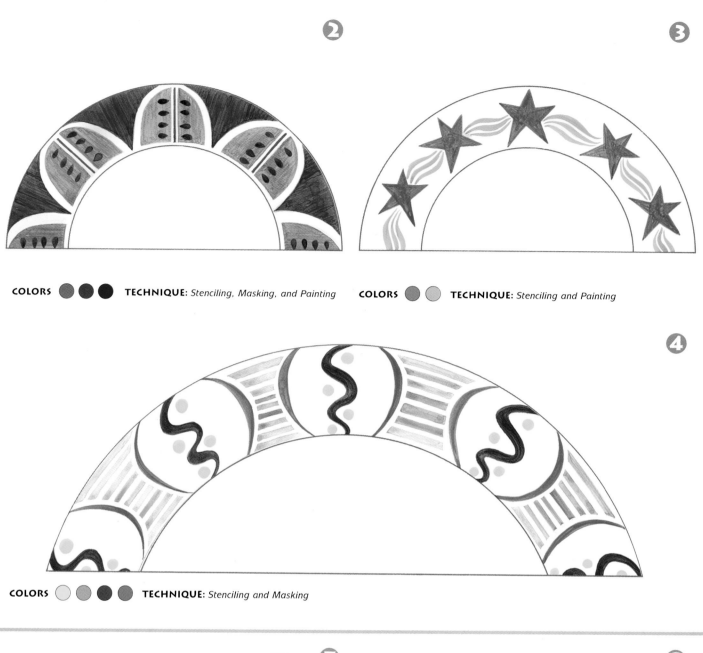

COLORS ● ● ● **TECHNIQUE:** *Stenciling, Masking, and Painting*

COLORS ● ● **TECHNIQUE:** *Stenciling and Painting*

COLORS ○ ● ● ● **TECHNIQUE:** *Stenciling and Masking*

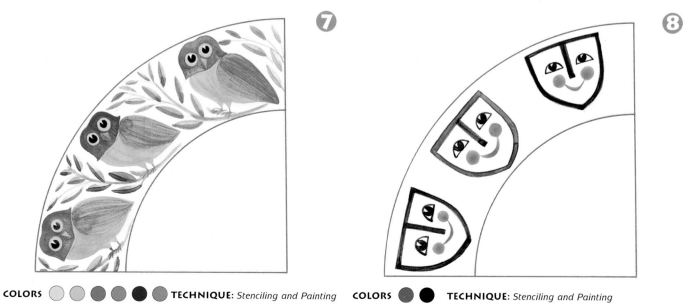

COLORS ○ ● ● ● ● ● **TECHNIQUE:** *Stenciling and Painting*

COLORS ● ● **TECHNIQUE:** *Stenciling and Painting*

LARGE, ROUND **PLATE**

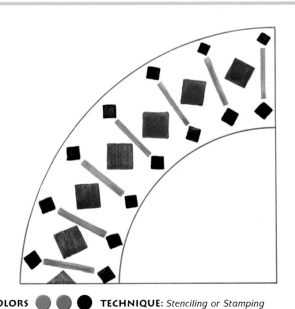

DESIGN 1 IS similar to a design from the previous section; the beauty of some of these designs is that you can transfer them from one object to another, making complete sets of crockery if you wish. The olives and tomatoes of Designs 2 and 6 lend themselves to being painted; the geometric pattern of Design 5 would look better stenciled. The animal print of Design 3 can be painted freely, but more precision is required for the pinks in Design 4. A sponged texture suits Design 7. The filled-in alphabet of Design 8 may require a little practice and patience.

1

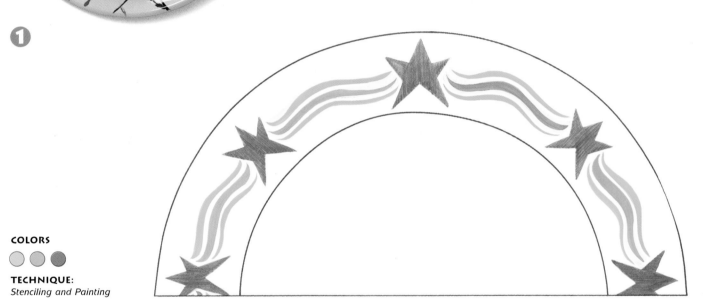

COLORS
⚪ ⚪ ⚫

TECHNIQUE:
Stenciling and Painting

5

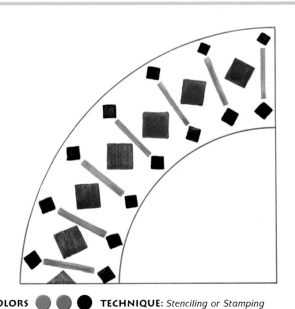

6

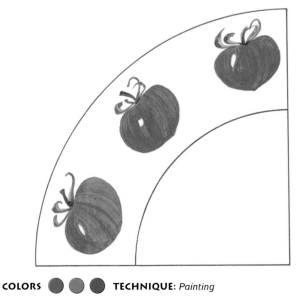

COLORS ⚫ ⚫ ⚫ **TECHNIQUE:** *Stenciling or Stamping*

COLORS ⚫ ⚫ ⚫ **TECHNIQUE:** *Painting*

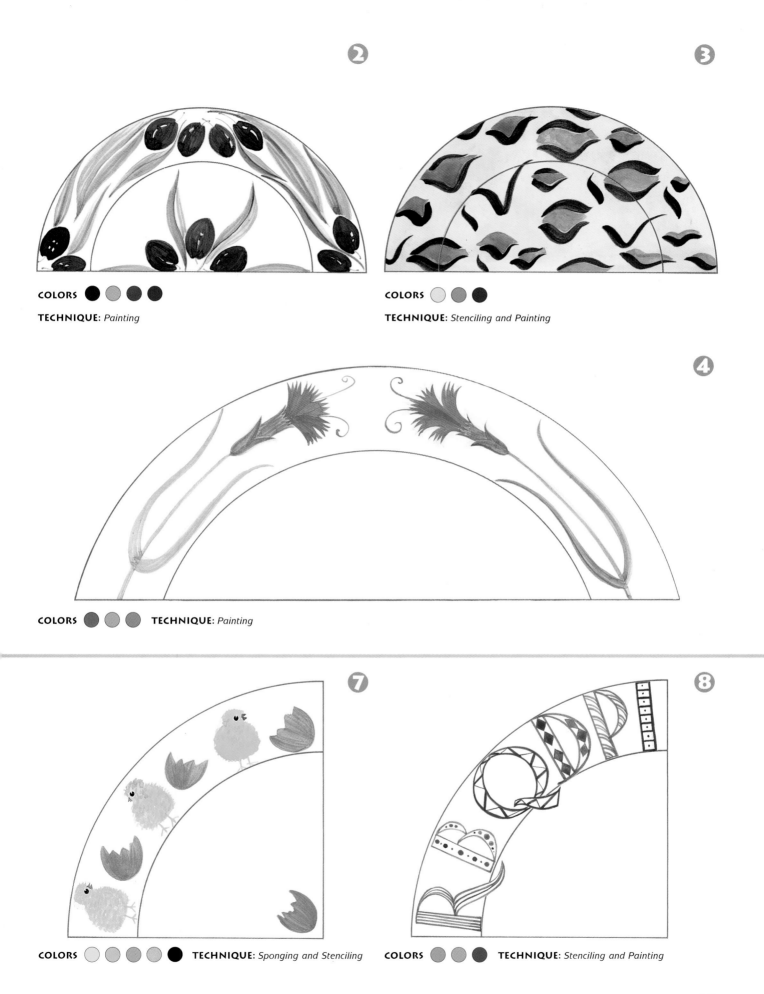

2

COLORS ● ● ● ●

TECHNIQUE: *Painting*

3

COLORS ● ● ●

TECHNIQUE: *Stenciling and Painting*

4

COLORS ● ● ●   **TECHNIQUE:** *Painting*

7

COLORS ● ● ● ● ●   **TECHNIQUE:** *Sponging and Stenciling*

8

COLORS ● ● ●   **TECHNIQUE:** *Stenciling and Painting*

SQUARE PLATES ARE *unusual and striking. Often they are ornamental rather than functional, so you can apply bold designs across the whole surface of the plate. Design 1 is easy to accomplish, and the*

tulips of Design 5 should not produce many problems either. A stencil would be useful for the geometric pattern of Design 2 and for Design 6. The dress, legs, and shoes of the flamenco dancer in Design 3 can be stenciled and the rest painted. Design 4, "Aries," could be stenciled, as could the curls and the border symbols. The tangerines of Design 7 could be stenciled and the center background sponged to give a contrasting texture, while the Christmas feel of Design 8 would look good stenciled and painted.

1

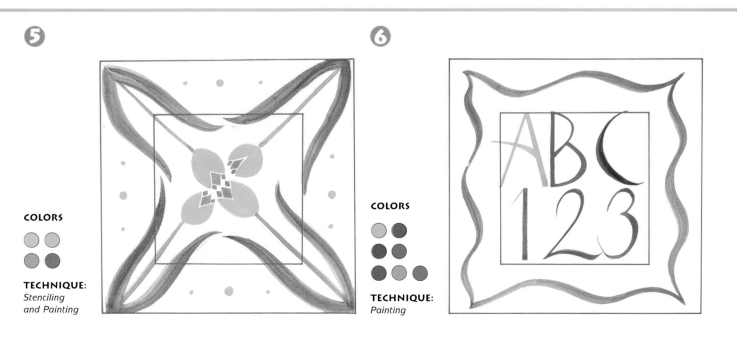

COLORS ⬤⬤⬤ **TECHNIQUE:** *Stenciling*

5

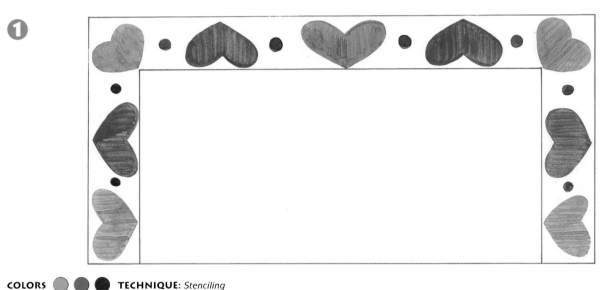

COLORS

TECHNIQUE:
*Stenciling
and Painting*

6

COLORS

TECHNIQUE:
Painting

2

COLORS  **TECHNIQUE:** *Masking and Stenciling*

3

COLORS

TECHNIQUE:
*Painting
and Stenciling*

4

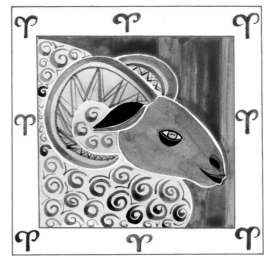

COLORS

TECHNIQUE:
*Stenciling,
Sponging,
and Stamping*

7

COLORS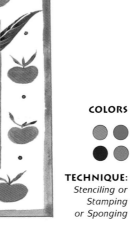

TECHNIQUE:
*Stenciling or
Stamping
or Sponging*

8

COLORS

TECHNIQUE:
*Stenciling,
Sponging,
and Painting*

HEXAGONAL **PLATES**

DESIGNS 1 AND 5 are fairly simple, using a combination of stenciling and painting. Design 2 requires a little patience; mask out a design or use a stencil. The intense, contrasting colors of Design 3 really make this plate stand out. In Design 4 we have hearts again, always popular, and very easy to do using a stencil. The clown face of Design 6 is easily achieved by use of stencil and painting, and looks wonderful in the hexagonal frame of the plate. Slightly more complicated is Design 7, but take it slowly and you will achieve the intended, striking result. An olive pattern graces Design 8.

①

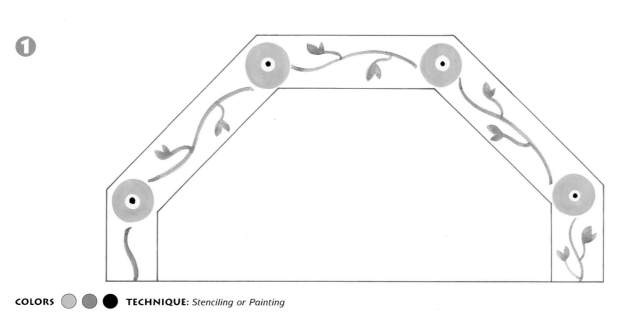

COLORS ⚪ 🔵 ⚫ **TECHNIQUE:** *Stenciling or Painting*

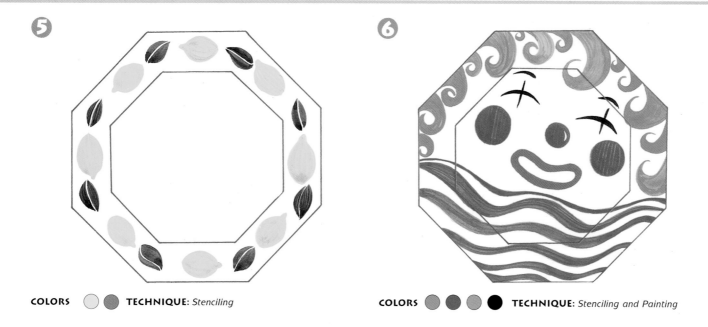

⑤

COLORS ⚪ 🔵 **TECHNIQUE:** *Stenciling*

⑥

COLORS 🔵 🔵 🔵 ⚫ **TECHNIQUE:** *Stenciling and Painting*

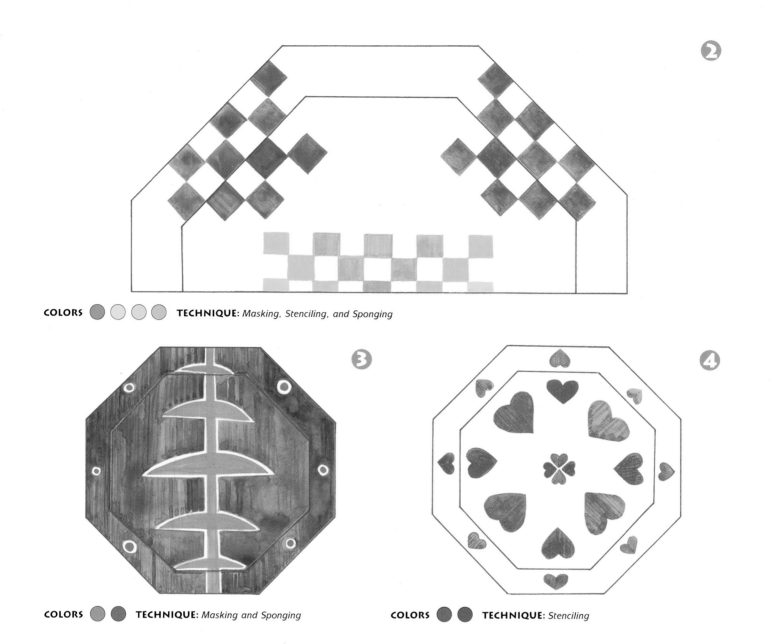

2

COLORS ⬤ ⬤ ⬤ ⬤ **TECHNIQUE:** *Masking, Stenciling, and Sponging*

3

COLORS ⬤ ⬤ **TECHNIQUE:** *Masking and Sponging*

4

COLORS ⬤ ⬤ **TECHNIQUE:** *Stenciling*

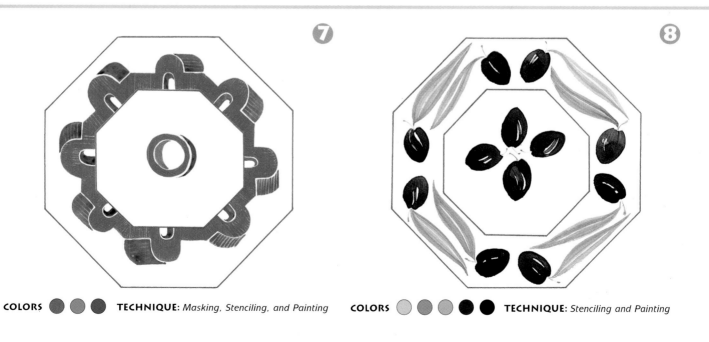

7

COLORS ⬤ ⬤ ⬤ **TECHNIQUE:** *Masking, Stenciling, and Painting*

8

COLORS ⬤ ⬤ ⬤ ⬤ ⬤ **TECHNIQUE:** *Stenciling and Painting*

103

ROUND **SERVING DISH/PLATTER**

ON SOME OF *these designs you will find there is extra space for decoration, namely the sides of the platter. Design 1 combines an upper and lower case alphabet. The fishes of Design 2, the geometric patterns of Design 7, the chilies of Design 8 and the flowers of Design 9 all suit stenciling and then sponging to give a contrasting texture. Designs 3 and 5 work well with stenciling and painting, while the snake in Design 4 looks good painted. The checked mask of Design 6 requires a combination of techniques: masking, stenciling, sponging, and painting.*

1

COLORS ● ● ● ● ● ● **TECHNIQUE:** *Painting*

6

7

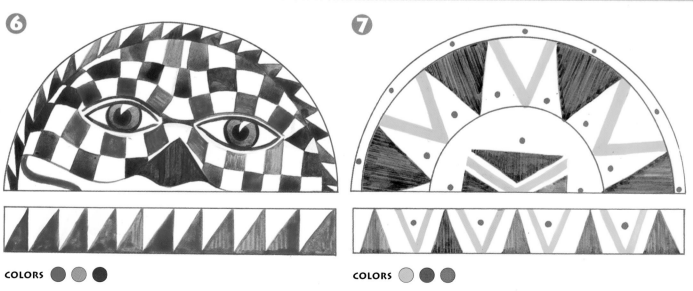

COLORS ● ● ●

TECHNIQUE: *Stenciling, Sponging, Masking, and Painting*

COLORS ● ● ●

TECHNIQUE: *Stenciling and Sponging*

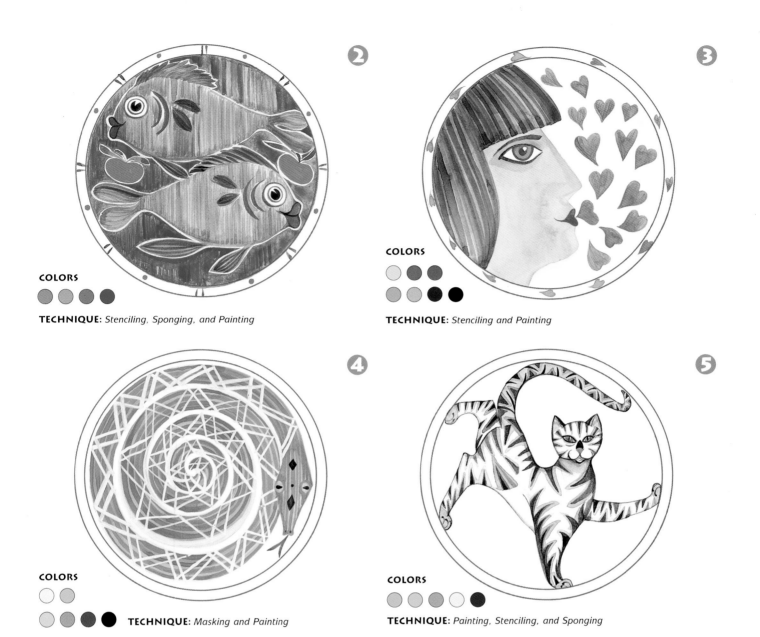

COLORS ●●●●

TECHNIQUE: *Stenciling, Sponging, and Painting*

COLORS ●●● ●●●●

TECHNIQUE: *Stenciling and Painting*

COLORS ●● ●●●●

TECHNIQUE: *Masking and Painting*

COLORS ●●●●●

TECHNIQUE: *Painting, Stenciling, and Sponging*

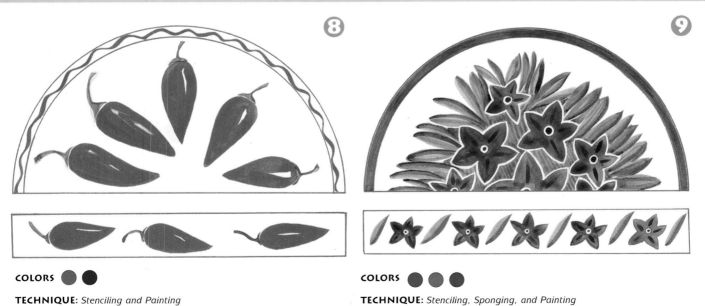

COLORS ●●

TECHNIQUE: *Stenciling and Painting*

COLORS ●●●

TECHNIQUE: *Stenciling, Sponging, and Painting*

OVAL **SERVING DISH/PLATTER**

THE CHRISTMAS THEME *in Design 1 can easily be created by stenciling and sponging. The curves and dots of Design 6 can be stenciled too. You will have to show some patience when you come to position the numbers of the clock in Design 2. The bold and smiling face of Design 3, perfect for this large dish, can be created with either a mask or a stencil. The Queen of Hearts in Design 4 uses a combination of stenciling and painting, as does Design 7. If you are feeling confident try Design 8, painting it free hand. The peppers and tomatoes of Design 9 make a colorful design—who needs the real thing when painted images look this good!*

1

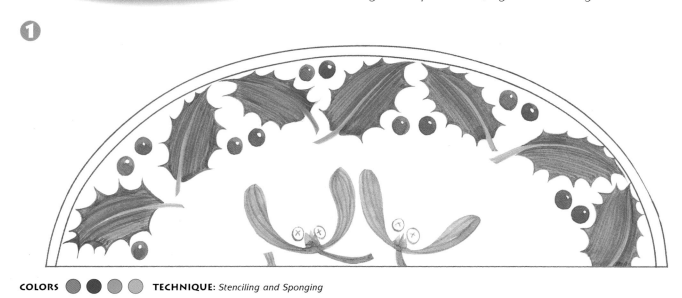

COLORS ○ ● ○ ○ **TECHNIQUE:** *Stenciling and Sponging*

6 **7**

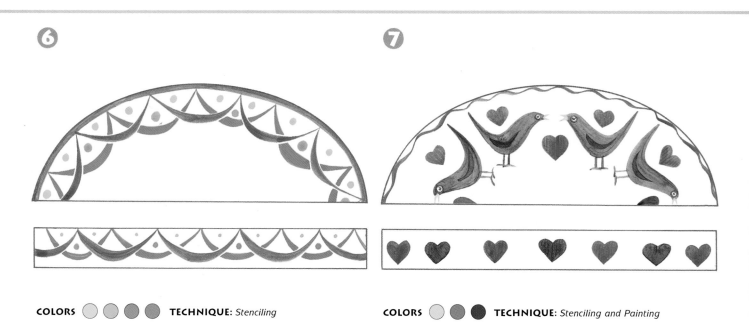

COLORS ○ ○ ● ● **TECHNIQUE:** *Stenciling*   **COLORS** ○ ○ ● ● **TECHNIQUE:** *Stenciling and Painting*

COLORS ⚪ ⚫ **TECHNIQUE:** *Stenciling and Painting*

COLORS 🔵🔵🔵 🔵🔵🔵🔵

TECHNIQUE: *Stenciling, Masking, and Sponging*

COLORS 🔵🔵🔵🔵 🔵🔵🔵🔵

TECHNIQUE: *Stenciling and Painting*

COLORS 🔵 🔵🔵

TECHNIQUE: *Painting, Stenciling, and Masking*

COLORS 🔵🔵🔵 **TECHNIQUE:** *Painting*

COLORS ⚪🔵🔵 **TECHNIQUE:** *Painting, Stenciling, and Masking*

107

SQUARE **SERVING DISH/PLATTER**

DESIGN 9, WITH *its stenciled flowers and diagonal wavy lines, should be the easiest in this section for the beginner to try. The robust shapes and colors of the chilies and peppers in Design 1, and the hand and stars of Design 3, are suited to stenciling and painting. The smiling clown of Design 2, the heart tree in Design 4, and the lizards in Design 8 can all be created by using stenciling and painting. The curves of Design 6 can be either masked or stenciled, while the swaying grasses of Design 7 call for some confident brushwork.*

①

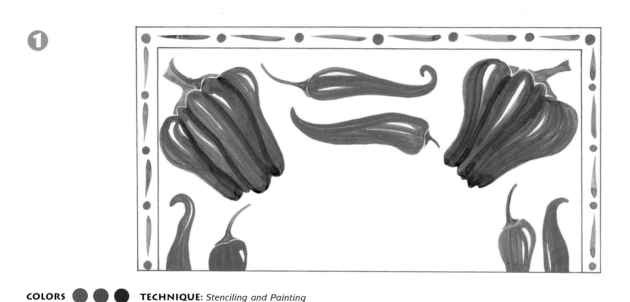

COLORS ● ● ●   **TECHNIQUE:** *Stenciling and Painting*

⑥   **⑦**

COLORS ● ● ●   **TECHNIQUE:** *Stenciling and Masking*   **COLORS** ● ● ● ● ● ● ● ●   **TECHNIQUE:** *Painting*

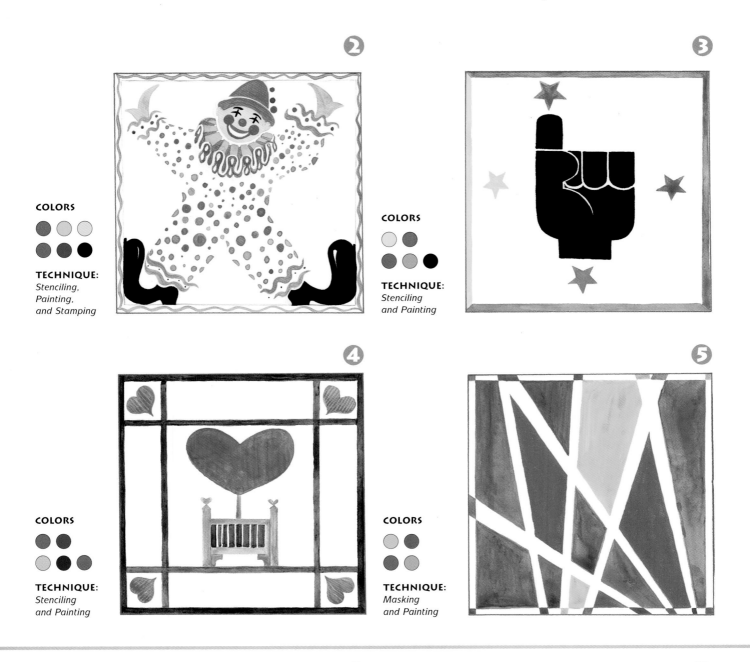

2

COLORS

TECHNIQUE:
*Stenciling,
Painting,
and Stamping*

3

COLORS

TECHNIQUE:
*Stenciling
and Painting*

4

COLORS

TECHNIQUE:
*Stenciling
and Painting*

5

COLORS

TECHNIQUE:
*Masking
and Painting*

8

COLORS **TECHNIQUE:** *Stenciling and Painting*

9

COLORS **TECHNIQUE:** *Stenciling and Painting*

RECTANGULAR /HEX **SERVING DISH**

THERE ARE MANY *colorful designs to choose from in this section, and Designs 1, 4, and 5 are good places for the beginner to start. Both the sweet little ballerina of Design 2 and the cherries of Design 3 look best painted. The tulips of Design 6 flow nicely across the dish. In the case of Design 7, you might need to practice the almost abstract hand and flower before you get the flow right. The flowers of Design 8 and the swans of Design 9 are definite candidates for stenciling or masking.*

1

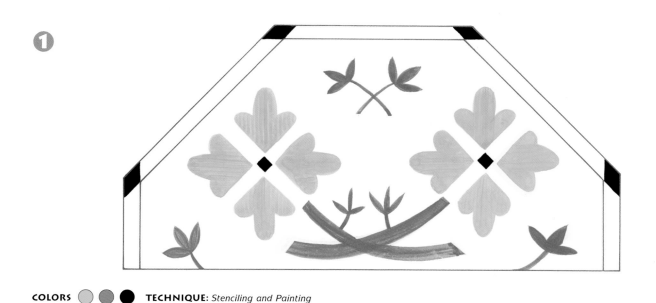

COLORS ⚪ ⚫ ⚫ **TECHNIQUE:** *Stenciling and Painting*

6

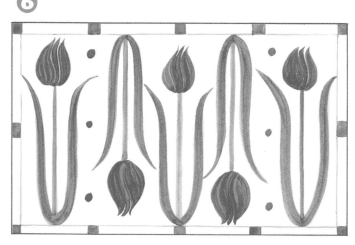

COLORS ⚫ ⚫ ⚫ **TECHNIQUE:** *Stenciling and Painting*

7

COLORS ⚪ ⚫ ⚫ ⚫ **TECHNIQUE:** *Painting*

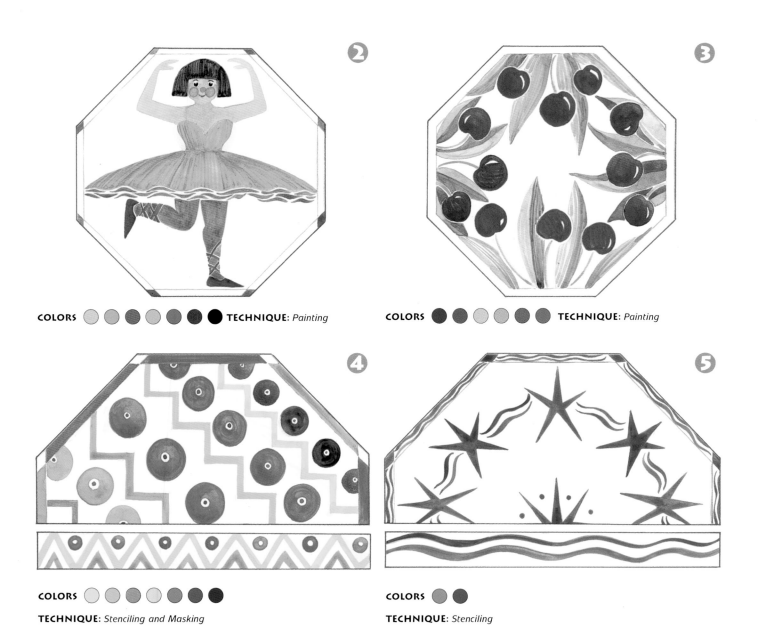

2

COLORS ⬤⬤⬤⬤⬤⬤⬤ **TECHNIQUE:** *Painting*

3

COLORS ⬤⬤⬤⬤⬤⬤⬤ **TECHNIQUE:** *Painting*

4

COLORS ⬤⬤⬤⬤⬤⬤⬤

TECHNIQUE: *Stenciling and Masking*

5

COLORS ⬤⬤

TECHNIQUE: *Stenciling*

8

COLORS ⬤⬤⬤⬤

TECHNIQUE: *Stenciling and Sponging or Painting*

9

COLORS ⬤⬤

TECHNIQUE: *Stenciling or Masking*

SQUARE **TILES/COASTERS**

THE GREAT THING *about tiles and coasters is that they are almost like blank canvases, just waiting to be painted! They are very versatile ceramic objects, and we use them to decorate many different areas of our homes. The blue hand of Design 1 and the fish of Design 4 can both be created by combining masking, stenciling, and painting. Many of these designs can be achieved by stenciling: the juicy strawberries of Design 2, the abstract of Design 5, the hearts of Design 6, the pinks of Design 7, the blackbirds of Design 8, the simple tulip of Design 9, and the lemons of Design 10. Design 3 will need careful masking to achieve those crisp edges.*

1

COLORS ● ● ● **TECHNIQUE:** *Masking, Stenciling, and Painting*

2

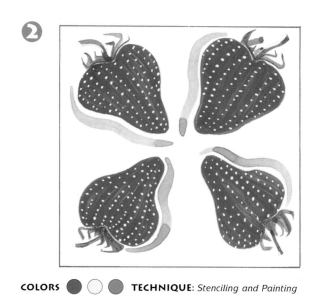

COLORS ● ○ ● **TECHNIQUE:** *Stenciling and Painting*

7

COLORS ● ● ● **TECHNIQUE:** *Stenciling*

8

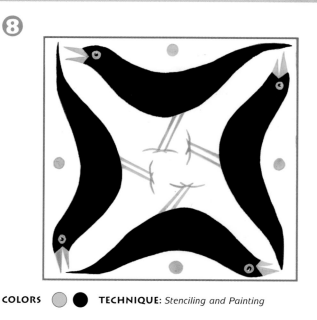

COLORS ● ● **TECHNIQUE:** *Stenciling and Painting*

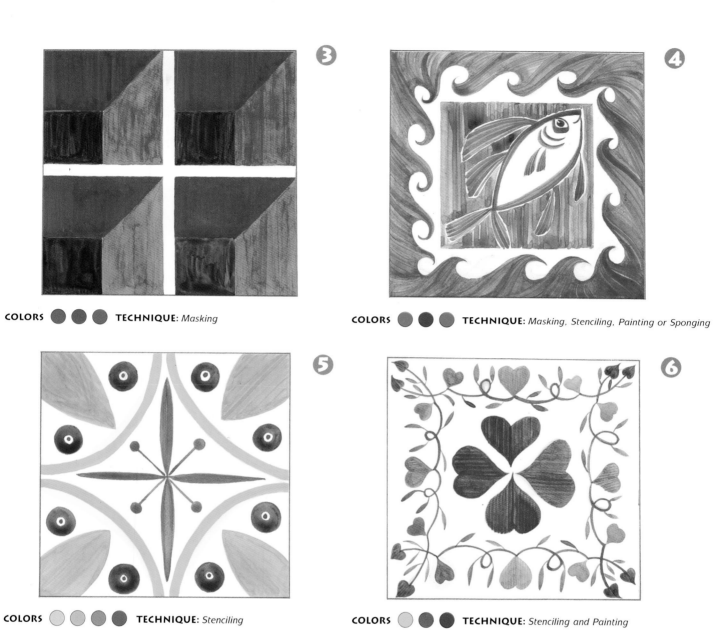

COLORS ● ● ● **TECHNIQUE:** *Masking*

COLORS ● ● ● **TECHNIQUE:** *Masking, Stenciling, Painting or Sponging*

COLORS ○ ● ● ● **TECHNIQUE:** *Stenciling*

COLORS ○ ● ● **TECHNIQUE:** *Stenciling and Painting*

COLORS ● ● ● **TECHNIQUE:** *Stenciling*

COLORS ○ ○ ● ● **TECHNIQUE:** *Stenciling and Sponging*

113

OTHER SHAPES OF **TILES/COASTERS**

DIFFERENT SHAPES INSPIRE *different ideas; when it comes to tiles and coasters, finding unusual shapes could inspire you to exploit them with unique designs. Here are some designs you may want to practice, many of them created by using a stencil: the hen of Design 1, the Yin and Yang symbol of Design 2, the trumps of Design 5, the blue star of Design 7, the sun, moon, and stars of Design 10. The texture of the oranges in Design 3 can be achieved by sponging, while the frog and tadpoles of Design 8 can be painted. Masking or sponging is appropriate for the abstract pattern of Design 4. The owl of Design 6 combines painting and stenciling.*

①

COLORS ●●●●● **TECHNIQUE:** *Stenciling and Painting*

②

COLORS ●● **TECHNIQUE:** *Stenciling or Masking and Sponging*

⑦

COLORS ●●● **TECHNIQUE:** *Stenciling, Masking, and Painting*

⑧

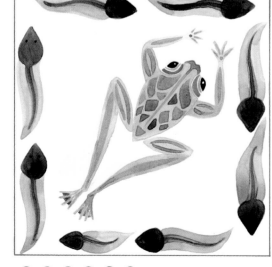

COLORS ●●●●●● **TECHNIQUE:** *Stenciling and Painting*

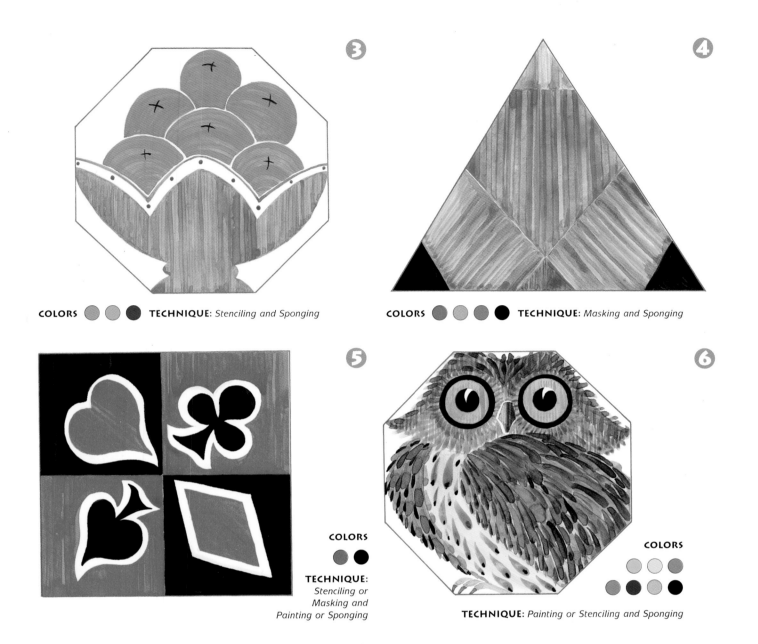

3

COLORS ⬤⬤⬤ **TECHNIQUE:** *Stenciling and Sponging*

4

COLORS ⬤⬤⬤⬤ **TECHNIQUE:** *Masking and Sponging*

5

COLORS ⬤⬤

TECHNIQUE:
*Stenciling or
Masking and
Painting or Sponging*

6

COLORS

⬤⬤⬤
⬤⬤⬤⬤

TECHNIQUE: *Painting or Stenciling and Sponging*

9

COLORS ⬤⬤⬤⬤ **TECHNIQUE:** *Stenciling and Painting*

10

COLORS ⬤⬤⬤⬤⬤⬤

TECHNIQUE: *Stenciling or Masking and Sponging*

THEMES 1 **CELEBRATIONS**

THE FOLLOWING SECTIONS *contain a wide range of ideas for borders and icons. Some of the designs have already been used in the book; here you can see how versatile they are. This first section covers celebrations and anniversaries. For Christmas we have the traditional holly and mistletoe, the Christmas tree and the snowman, the crackers, and the pudding. To mark Easter there is an Easter chick and Easter eggs. The bells, cake, and presents are to help you celebrate the next wedding you attend. The Halloween pumpkins are great fun.*

COLORS

TECHNIQUE:
*Stenciling
and Painting*

COLORS

TECHNIQUE:
*Stenciling and
Painting*

COLORS

TECHNIQUE:
*Stenciling and
Sponging*

COLORS

TECHNIQUE: *Stenciling
and Sponging*

COLORS

TECHNIQUE:
*Stenciling and
Sponging
or Painting*

COLORS

TECHNIQUE: *Stenciling*

COLORS

TECHNIQUE:
Stenciling and Painting

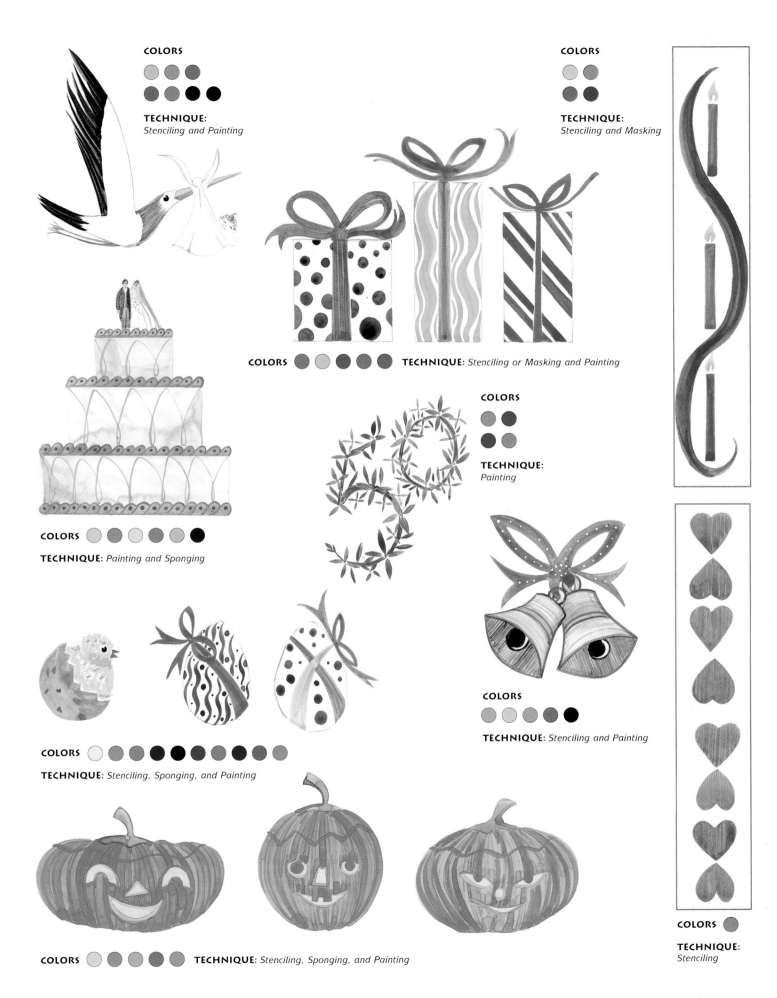

COLORS

TECHNIQUE:
Stenciling and Painting

COLORS

TECHNIQUE:
Stenciling and Masking

COLORS **TECHNIQUE:** *Stenciling or Masking and Painting*

COLORS

TECHNIQUE:
Painting

COLORS

TECHNIQUE: *Painting and Sponging*

COLORS

TECHNIQUE: *Stenciling and Painting*

COLORS

TECHNIQUE: *Stenciling, Sponging, and Painting*

COLORS **TECHNIQUE:** *Stenciling, Sponging, and Painting*

COLORS

TECHNIQUE:
Stenciling

117

THERE'S A GREAT *variety of New Age and zodiac designs and decoration to choose from, and in this section you should find ideas to inspire you. Zodiac themes range from the glyphs (ornamental symbols) on the border representing Earth, Air, Fire, and Water, to the symbols for birth signs and the planets. You may recognize some of the designs from earlier in the book, and the borders of trumps and stars will be familiar. Of the many tarot card symbols we have selected only a few.*

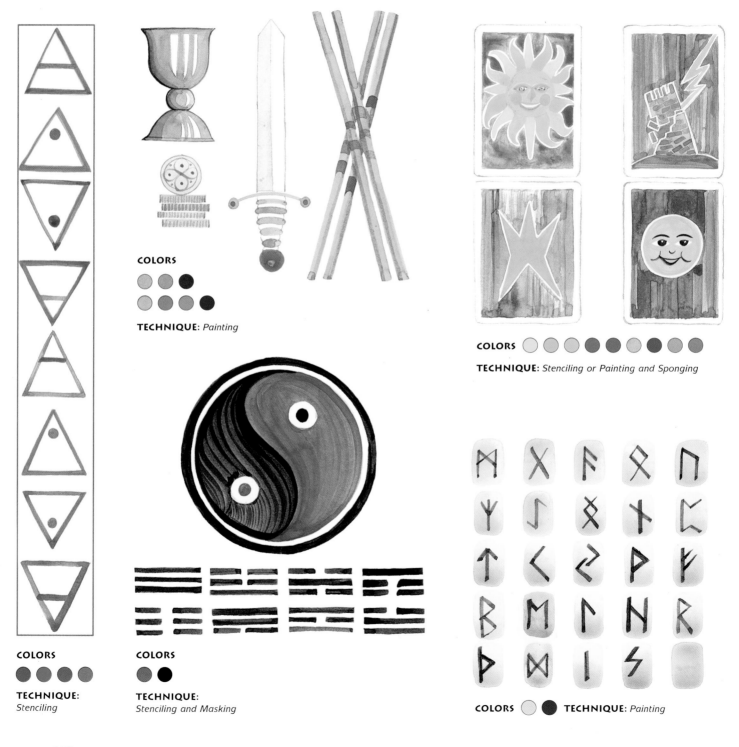

COLORS

TECHNIQUE: *Painting*

COLORS

TECHNIQUE: *Stenciling or Painting and Sponging*

COLORS

TECHNIQUE:
Stenciling

COLORS

TECHNIQUE:
Stenciling and Masking

COLORS **TECHNIQUE:** *Painting*

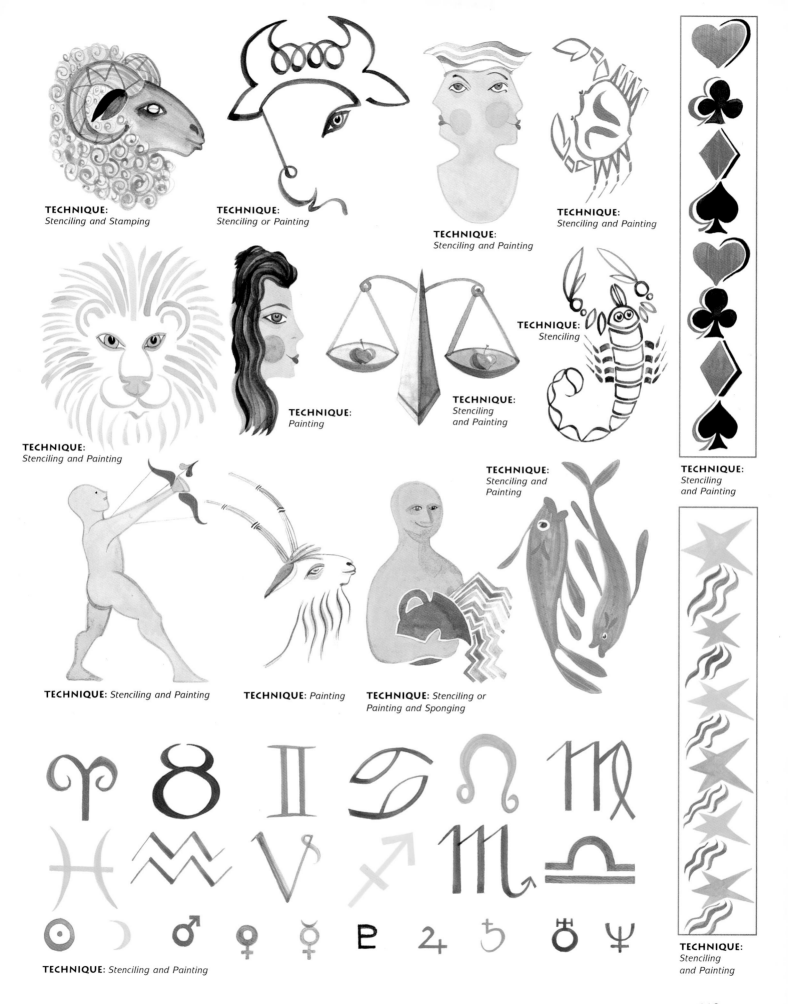

TECHNIQUE:
Stenciling and Stamping

TECHNIQUE:
Stenciling or Painting

TECHNIQUE:
Stenciling and Painting

TECHNIQUE:
Stenciling and Painting

TECHNIQUE:
Stenciling and Painting

TECHNIQUE:
Painting

TECHNIQUE:
Stenciling

TECHNIQUE:
Stenciling and Painting

TECHNIQUE:
Stenciling and Painting

TECHNIQUE:
Stenciling and Painting

TECHNIQUE: *Stenciling and Painting*

TECHNIQUE: *Painting*

TECHNIQUE: *Stenciling or Painting and Sponging*

TECHNIQUE: *Stenciling and Painting*

TECHNIQUE:
Stenciling and Painting

119

ALPHABETS AND NUMBERS *make pleasing designs on ceramics. There are so many different typefaces to choose from, and by using instant lettering sheets you should have no trouble creating stencils or masks for these designs. The Greek or Cyrillic alphabets can be used decoratively, as can the writing and alphabets of the cultures of India, China, Japan, and many more. There are some wonderful examples of calligraphy created by artists within the tradition of Islam. Roman numerals can also look very effective, as can simple repetition such as that present in the borders on page 121.*

TECHNIQUE:
Stenciling and Painting

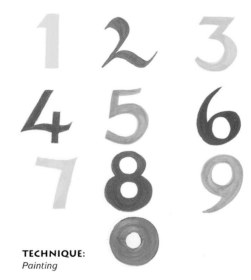

TECHNIQUE:
Painting

TECHNIQUE:
Painting

TECHNIQUE: *Painting or Stenciling*

TECHNIQUE: *Painting or Stenciling*

TECHNIQUE: *Painting or Stenciling*

ABCDEFGH
IJKLMNOP
QRSTUVW
XYZ

TECHNIQUE:
Stenciling and Painting

abcdefghijk
lmnopqrstuv
wxyz

TECHNIQUE:
Stenciling and Painting

ABCDEFGh
IJKLMNO
PQRSTUVW
XYZ

TECHNIQUE:
Stenciling or Painting

TECHNIQUE:
*Stenciling
or Painting*

TECHNIQUE:
*Stenciling
and Painting*

121

THEMES 4 **ANIMALS**

ANIMALS AND BIRDS *have always been a popular choice as decoration for ceramics, and throughout history the diversity of cultures has generated many styles of animal representation. One has only to think of the delicacy in the designs of Persian miniatures, or the free interpretation of animals that occurs in African tribal art. Many animals and birds have already appeared in this book; here are some new ones and some familiar ones. The lizards and snakes on the borders give a great sense of movement. Animals from the Chinese zodiac are also shown.*

COLORS

TECHNIQUE: *Stenciling and Painting*

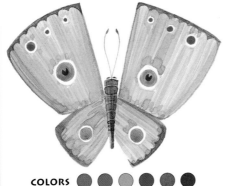

COLORS ● ● ● ● ● ●

TECHNIQUE:
Stenciling and Painting or Sponging

COLORS ● ●

TECHNIQUE: *Stenciling, Sponging, and Painting*

COLORS ● ● ● ●

TECHNIQUE: *Stenciling, Sponging, and Painting*

COLORS ● ● ● ●

TECHNIQUE: *Stenciling and Stamping*

COLORS ● ●

TECHNIQUE:
Painting or Stenciling and Sponging

COLORS ○ ○
● ●

TECHNIQUE:
Stenciling or Painting and Sponging

COLORS ● ○ ● ○ ● ●

TECHNIQUE:
Stenciling and Sponging or Painting

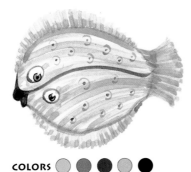

COLORS ● ● ● ● ●

TECHNIQUE:
Stenciling and Painting or Stamping or Sponging

COLORS ● ● ●

TECHNIQUE:
Painting

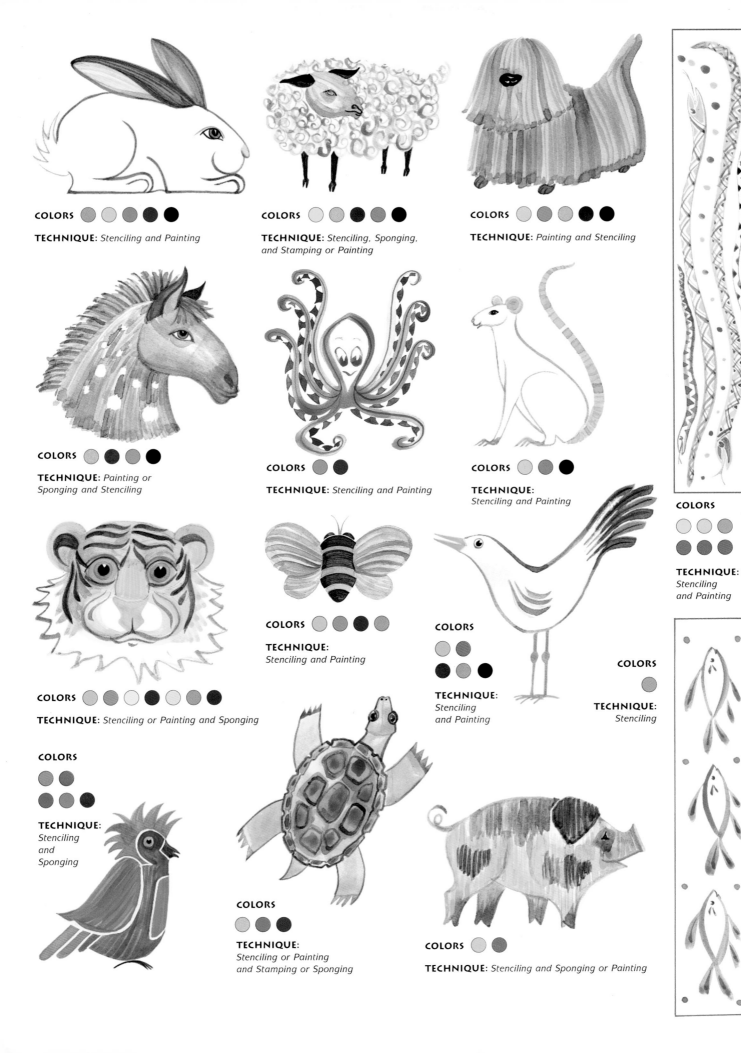

COLORS ● ● ● ● ●
TECHNIQUE: *Stenciling and Painting*

COLORS ● ● ● ● ●
TECHNIQUE: *Stenciling, Sponging, and Stamping or Painting*

COLORS ● ● ● ● ●
TECHNIQUE: *Painting and Stenciling*

COLORS ● ● ● ●
TECHNIQUE: *Painting or Sponging and Stenciling*

COLORS ● ●
TECHNIQUE: *Stenciling and Painting*

COLORS ● ● ●
TECHNIQUE: *Stenciling and Painting*

COLORS ● ● ●
● ● ●
TECHNIQUE: *Stenciling and Painting*

COLORS ● ● ● ● ● ● ●
TECHNIQUE: *Stenciling or Painting and Sponging*

COLORS ● ● ● ●
TECHNIQUE: *Stenciling and Painting*

COLORS ● ●
● ● ●
TECHNIQUE: *Stenciling and Painting*

COLORS ●
TECHNIQUE: *Stenciling*

COLORS ● ●
● ● ●
TECHNIQUE: *Stenciling and Sponging*

COLORS ● ● ●
TECHNIQUE: *Stenciling or Painting and Stamping or Sponging*

COLORS ● ●
TECHNIQUE: *Stenciling and Sponging or Painting*

THEMES 5 **FLOWERS, FRUIT & VEG**

FLOWERS, FRUIT, AND *vegetables are the mainstay of much ceramic decoration. All of the designs shown here have appeared in the book with the exception of the little group of beans. Products from our stores and plants from our backyards can seem so familiar, but if we stop taking them for granted and start to look at them more closely then they can be inspiring. We can interpret them as simply or as realistically as the mood takes us; the decorations we create from them enhance our everyday lives.*

TECHNIQUE: *Painting and Sponging*

TECHNIQUE: *Stenciling and Painting*

TECHNIQUE:
Stenciling and Painting

TECHNIQUE:
Stenciling and Sponging

TECHNIQUE:
Stenciling and Painting

TECHNIQUE:
Stenciling and Painting

TECHNIQUE:
Stenciling and Sponging

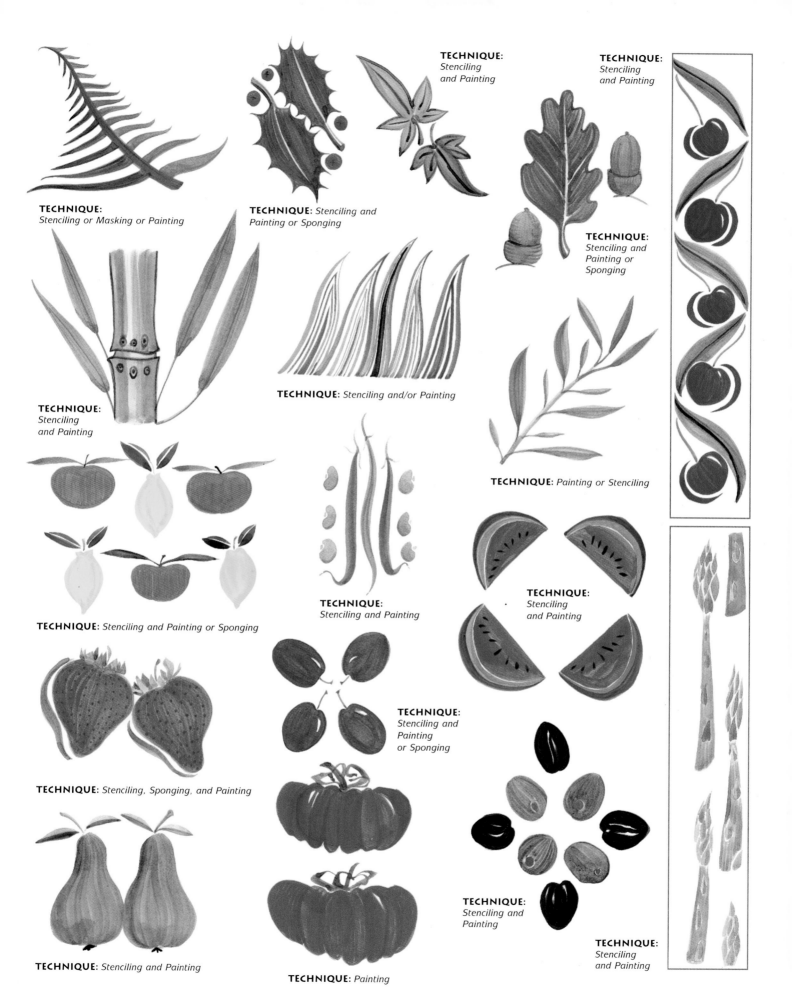

TECHNIQUE: *Stenciling or Masking or Painting*

TECHNIQUE: *Stenciling and Painting or Sponging*

TECHNIQUE: *Stenciling and Painting*

TECHNIQUE: *Stenciling and Painting*

TECHNIQUE: *Stenciling and Painting or Sponging*

TECHNIQUE: *Stenciling and/or Painting*

TECHNIQUE: *Painting or Stenciling*

TECHNIQUE: *Stenciling and Painting*

TECHNIQUE: *Stenciling and Painting or Sponging*

TECHNIQUE: *Stenciling, Sponging, and Painting*

TECHNIQUE: *Stenciling and Painting*

TECHNIQUE: *Stenciling and Painting or Sponging*

TECHNIQUE: *Stenciling and Painting*

TECHNIQUE: *Stenciling and Painting*

TECHNIQUE: *Stenciling and Painting*

TECHNIQUE: *Painting*

TECHNIQUE: *Stenciling and Painting*

125

SUPPLIERS

UNITED KINGDOM

British Ceramic Federation
Federation House
Station Road
STOKE on TRENT
Staffordshire ST4 2SA
tel: 01782 744 631
fax: 01782 744 102

Pottery Crafts (HQ)
Campbell Road
STOKE on TRENT
Staffordshire ST4 4ET
tel: 01782 745 000
fax: 01782 746 000

Pottery Crafts London
8-10 Ingate Place
BATTERSEA
London SW8 3NS
tel: 0171 720 0050
fax: 0171 627 8290

Pebeo [UK}
Unit 416 Solent Business Centre
Millbrook Road West
MILLBROOK
Southampton SO15 OHW
tel: 01703 901 914/915
fax: 01703 901 916

Liquitex
Winsor and Newton
Whitefriars Avenue
WEALDSTONE
Harrow HAJ 5RH
tel: 0181 427 4343

UNITED STATES

Pebeo of America
Route 78, Airport Road
PO Box 714
SWANTON
Vermont 05488
tel: (819) 829 5012
fax: (819) 821 4151

Dunham Ceramics
2870 Milburn Avenue
BALDWIN
Long Island 11510
tel: (516) 223 0642

Ro's Ceramic Supply
Teall Avenue
SYRACUSE
New York 13206
tel: 1 800 864 0511

T & D Ceramics
2133-2135 Broadway
BUFFALO
New York 14212
tel: (716) 894 9209

Baro's Ceramic Supply
114 Gorham Street
CHELMSFORD
Massachusetts 01824
tel: (508) 441 2400

Hatton Ceramics
212 Washington Avenue
LITTLE FERRY
New Jersey 07643

Central Florida Ceramic Supply
6566 University Boulevard
WINTER PARK
Florida 32792
tel: (407) 657 5752

Dunham Ceramics South
912 S.E. 8th Place
CAPE CORAL
Florida 33990
tel: (813) 574 2226

Charlene's Ceramics & Supplies
3409 W. 63rd Street
CHICAGO
Illinois 60629
tel: (312) 737 9220

A.B. Ceramics
307 South Fourth Street
JEANETTE
Pennsylvania 15644
tel: (412) 523 5943

American Ceramic Supply Company
2442 Ludelle
FORT WORTH
Texas 76105
tel: (817) 536 7120

Ceramic Art Distributors
7576 Clairmont Mesa Blvd
Suite A
SAN DIEGO
California 92154
tel: (909) 627 4139

Ceramic & Craft Warehouse, Inc
13595 12th Street
CHINO
California 91710
tel: (909) 627 4139

All About Ceramics
4375 Bay Road
BLAINE
Washington 98230
tel: (206) 371 2411

Artistic Ceramic Shops
10201 W. Oklahama Avenue
MILWAUKEE
Wisconsin 53227
tel: (414) 321 1144

CANADA

Lynwood Ceramics Ltd
246 Westbrook Road
OTTAWA
Ontario K2K 1X4
tel: (613) 831 1250

Old Mill Ceramics
RR 3
BRIGHTON
Ontario K0K 1H0
tel: (613) 475 1144

AUSTRALIA

Melton Ceramic Supplies
11 Production Road
MELTON
Victoria 3337
tel: (03) 743 9479

Reward Ceramic Products
6 Goongarrie Street
BAYSWATER
Western Australia 6053
tel: (09) 378 1322

Ellen Massey Porcelain
439-441 West Botany Street
KOGARAH
NSW 2217
tel: (02) 553 9475

INDEX

All techniques and themes are illustrated; page numbers in italics indicate illustrations not referred to in text.

A
adhesive tape 10
alphabets 120-1
animals, as themes 122-3
astrology, as theme 118

B
baking 8, 16
beakers, straight-sided 36-7
birds, as themes 122-3
boats and saucers 64-5
bowls:
    cone 44-5
    large salad/fruit 46-7
    large, shallow 48-9
    lipped 40-1
    sugar, round 38-9
    unlipped 42-3
brushes 10, 11, 16-17
butter dishes 86-7

C
carbon paper 10, 13
Causeway Bay, Hong Kong 7
celebrations, themes for 116-17
cheese dishes 88-9
Christmas, themes for 106, 116
coasters:
    square 112-13
    other shapes 114-15
coffee-pot, straight-sided 62-3
color wheel 23
colors:
    complementary 23
    cool 23
    test firing 9
    tones 23
    warm 23
compasses 10

containers 10
cotton swabs 10
cruet set 78-9
cups and saucers:
    rounded 24-7
    straight-sided 28-9
cutting 14
cutting board/mat 10

D
designs:
    adapting 6
    in color 23
    re-sizing 12
    transferring 13
dishes:
    butter 86-7
    cheese 88-9
    roasting, large 92-3
    serving:
        hexagonal 110-11
        oval 106-7
        rectangular 110-11
        round 104-5
        square 108-9
dotwork 22
drying 16

E
Easter, themes for 116, 117
eggcups 76-7
equipment 10-11

F
fiber-tipped pen 10
firing 8
flowers, as themes 124
fruit, as themes 124, 125
fruit bowls, large 46-7

G
graph paper 10
gravy boats and saucers 64-5
grid, re-sizing with 12

H
hairdryer 16
Hallowe'en, themes for 116, 117
Hong Kong 7

J
jugs:
    large 52-3
    small 50-1
    straight-sided 54-5

K
kilns 8
    loading 8

L
lettering, as theme 120-1
Lily Acapulco 7

M
masking 15-16
masking film/paper 10, 16
masking liquid 10, 15
masking tape 10, 16
materials 10-11
methylated spirit 11
modelling clay 11
mugs:
    cone 34-5
    curved 32-3
    straight-sided 30-1
Musée d'Orsay, Paris 6
mustard pots 80-1

N
New Age, themes for 118-19
numbers, as themes 120

O
ovens see kilns

P
painting, techniques 16-17
paints:
    consistency 16
    diluting 8
    solvent-based 8-9
    testing for dryness 16
    thinning 16
    water-based 8-9
palette 11
paper:
    carbon 10, 13
    graph 10
    tracing 11, 12, 13
pencils 11
pens 10
photocopying 12
pitchers:
    large 52-3
    straight-sided 54-5
planters 74-5
plates:
    hexagonal 102-3
    large, round 98-9
    medium, round 96-7
    small, round 94-5
    square 100-1
platters:
    oval 106-7
    round 104-5
    square 108-9

R
re-sizing designs 12
roasting dishes, large 92-3
ruler 11

S
safety 8
salad bowls, large 46-7
salt and pepper sets 78-9
sauce boats and saucers 64-5
scalpel 11
scissors 11
serving dishes:
    hexagonal 110-11
    oval 106-7
    rectangular 110-11

serving dishes *(cont'd)*:
   round 104-5
   square 108-9
sgraffito 22
sketch pad 11
spattering 20
spice jars, small, lidded 82-3
sponges 11, 20
sponging 20
stamping 21
stamps:
   rubber 21
   sponge 21
stencil cardboard 11
stenciling 18-19
stencils, cutting 18-19
storage jars:
   large, lidded 84-5
   small, lidded 82-3
string 11
sugar bowls, round 38-9

T

tape measure 11
teapots:
   round 56-9
   straight-sided 60-1
techniques 14-23
templates, using 12-13
themes 116-25
   alphabets 120-1
   animals 122-3
   astrology 118-19
   celebrations 116-17
   flowers 124
   fruit 124, 125
   lettering 120-1
   New Age 118
   vegetables 124, 125
tiles:
   square 112-13
   other shapes 114-15
tips 14
tissue 11
toothbrush 11
tracing paper 11, 12, 13
transferring design 13
tureens, round 90-1
turntable 11
turpentine 11

V

vases:
   cone 70-1
   large, curved 68-9
   small, curved 66-7
   tall, shaped 72-3
vegetable tureens, round 90-1
vegetables, as themes 124, 125

W

weddings, themes for 116, 117

CREDITS

Quarto Publishing plc would like to thank the following ceramic artists for kindly supplying us with samples of their work to appear in this book:

Scott Blades
The Kew Ceramics Cafe
1A Mortlake Terrace
Mortlake Road
Kew
Surrey TW9 3DT

Kate Byrne
Pond Farm Cottage
Holton
Oxfordshire OX33 1PY

Daphne Carnegy
Kingsgate Workshops
110-116 Kingsgate Road
London NW6 2JG

Sharon Clark
The Kew Ceramics Cafe
1A Mortlake Terrace
Mortlake Road
Kew
Surrey TW9 3DT

Ornella Galluccio
Genevra Jolley
The Brush 'N' Bisque-it
77 Church Road
Barnes
London SW13 9HH

Kate Glanville
Farmers
Bethlehem
Carmarthenshire SA199BS

Steven Jenkins
The Kew Ceramics Cafe
1A Mortlake Terrace
Mortlake Road
Kew, Surrey TW9 3DT

Mike Levy
6 Victoria Street
Brighton BN1 3FP

Sue Masters
Chasefield
50 Portway
Wells, Somerset BA5 2BW

John Pollex
White Lane Gallery
1 White Lane
Barbican
Plymouth, Devon PL1 2LP

Gaynor Reeve
Callis Court
London Road
West Malling
Kent ME19 5AH

Chris Speyer
Yerja Ceramics
Mill Rise
Ford Road
Brampton
Devon EX16 9LW

Sue Taylor
The Kew Ceramics Cafe
1A Mortlake Terrace
Mortlake Road
Kew
Surrey TW9 3DT

Simon Thomason
Thomason-Michel Ceramics
37 Mill Road
Lewes
East Sussex BN7 2RU

Jo Wood
The Kew Ceramics Cafe
1A Mortlake Terrace
Mortlake Road
Kew, Surrey TW9 3DT